Nancy Harris, Portrait of Max Weitzenhoffer.
Oil on canvas. 2003.

Max's Favorite Productions

Dracula

Firstly, to be virtually born on Halloween and from the time I read *Dracula* around the 7th grade, I have always been enamored of him. The movie with Bela Lugosi always made the Halloween rounds in OKC, and to this day is still a classic. Furthermore, I have 13 letters in my last name and always have had an association and belief in the occult and ghosts. So, the idea of doing the show stirred my BLOOD.

The Will Rogers Follies

This one, of course, goes without saying. Everything about the show from the dream team creating it to the very personal Oklahoma story line was perhaps my most thrilling experience. The whole creating team was "The A Team" and was never to be assembled again. Coupled with my late wife's illness and insistence I do it made it the most exciting and, in some ways, the most tragic experience of my career.

Song and Dance

I saw the show in London with Marti Webb in 1982 and the first part— *Tell me on a Sunday*—had a beautiful score and the second half—the *Dance* portion—was thrilling. The opportunity to work with Andrew in New York was my real break.

Aspects of Love

I found not only what I think was Andrews's most beautiful score but the subject of love being the key. And the sexual mores of love of a young soldier, an actress and his uncle in France touched all the things that a Puritan America cannot accept, but that I adore.

TO THE MAX

MAX WEITZENHOFFER'S MAGICAL TRIP FROM OKLAHOMA
TO NEW YORK AND LONDON—AND BACK

TOM LINDLEY

© 2019 Tom Lindley

Published by Full Circle Press
a division of Full Circle Bookstore LLC
1900 North West Expressway
Oklahoma City, Oklahoma 73118

Text is composed in Perpetua, a transitional typeface
designed by Eric Gill around 1925 and does not
reference any historic model. The display typeface is
Gill Sans, also by Eric Gill.

Book, text, and jacket by Carl Brune

Printed in China

First edition. First printing

ISBN 978-0-9858651-6-0

Men like my father cannot die. They are with me still, real in memory as they were in the flesh, loving and beloved forever. How green was my valley then.

— HOW GREEN WAS MY VALLEY, 1941

CONTENTS

Max Weitzenhoffer's name has never made the headlines but a lot of headlines wouldn't have been made without him. When you read most biographies of men who have made it big on Broadway they usually start with their struggle from New York's lower East Side.

Max's story is unique in that he had a privileged upbringing; on the walls of his home in Oklahoma you would find a Monet here or a Picasso there. He could have led a comfortable easy life but his father's oil business never really caught his attention. It was the world of theatre that got his juices flowing and this interest turned into a passion and finally an obsession.

We became good friends when he produced *Song and Dance*, a musical I wrote with Andrew Lloyd Webber. Max spent a lot of his youth going to the cinema and those early picture going memories are still with him today. In a Max Weitzenhoffer perfect world James Stewart would still be the local sheriff, James Cagney would be shouting "Top of the world, Ma," Rita Hayworth would be singing a wistful ballad in a noisy saloon and John Wayne would still be saving God-fearing farmers from ruthless outlaws.

Max has always been a dreamer and like most dreamers part of him has never left the playground. He loves a good laugh and doesn't like to spend much time talking about failure. He is always quickly on to the next hurdle and challenge. He is quietly spoken and charming and curious and cultivated. Try and imagine what David Niven would be like if he were born in Oklahoma City, Oklahoma.

A few years ago at his lavish 60th birthday party, which was held at London's Savoy Hotel, I wrote a poem for him which I've adjusted a little but hardly anything about him has changed.

—— DON BLACK

He was born in Oklahoma
In the year of '39
He should have been an oil man
Or the Foreman of some mine
While he sipped his tall mint juleps
'Neath those oleander trees
He used to dream of Broadway
And those Russian Tea Room teas
So he sacrificed his stetson
Black-eyed peas and candied yams
For lunches with the Schuberts
And New York traffic jams
Now his name's above the title
On many Broadway plays
But he can still talk for hours
About pistols and Monets
You can bet each time you see him
I would say that it's a cert
He will have a yellow tie on
A Turnbull and Asser shirt
If you want to get to know this dreamer
With the faraway look
The only way you'll do it
Is to go and buy this book
He's won his share of Tonys
Accolades and plaques
And when you read his bio
You will love him To The Max.

La Jolla Summer Playhouse. For me, it meant the constant association with all those wonderful movie stars of the day, although most of it was on a very limited basis. We have rock stars and movie stars today, but we don't have real stars anymore who were accessible to the public. You have a lot of little pieces in life that you keep, and La Jolla was a big piece of the puzzle that made me come out the way I am.

Mel Ferrer, Dorothy McGuire and Gregory Peck founded the playhouse in La Jolla, California. It became more than just a quiet getaway for the stars of the 1940s and '50s. It became a place to hone their craft in the company of some of the finest actors of the day. Courtesy the La Jolla Playhouse

Playhouse

First came the movies, then popcorn and concession stands and 3-D, all of it culminating just in time to seize on the euphoria of post-World War II America. By the late 1940s, the heavy churn of westerns, war heroes, monsters from the deep and cops and robbers had captured the imagination of one highly impressionable set of moviegoers in particular—kids. But in the case of a young Max Weitzenhoffer, the big screen devoured him as if he were an audience of one.

The only child of Aaron and Clara Weitzenhoffer of Oklahoma City, Oklahoma, Aaron Max Weitzenhoffer Jr. spent more time alone than most children, so it was a good thing his parents had the financial means to keep him entertained. There was some concern when movie ticket prices jumped from a dime to a quarter, limiting Max's Hershey bar consumption. Fortunately, that wasn't a problem on Sundays as that was the day Max's father took him to the movies. Randolph Scott was his father's favorite cowboy. The son idolized John Wayne.

No matter where you went in Oklahoma City in those days, there was not a shortage of theatres. It felt like there was one for every kernel of popcorn: elaborate and fanciful palaces such as the Criterion, the Shrine, the Warner and the Midwest Downtown, as well as the more evocatively named Tower, Log Cabin, Chieftain, Bison and many others elsewhere. The grandest of them all, The Will Rogers Theatre, opened on Sept. 18, 1946, ushering in a new era of luxury and comfort. Named for Oklahoma's favorite son, it offered theatre seating on an incline and could hold an audience of 1,000. Incredibly detailed murals that documented Rogers' life lined the walls and an 18-foot mural of the famed humorist, writer, roper and actor was the centerpiece of the lobby.

Double features were standard fare for the day. Even better, many single-screen theatres changed feature films twice a week. This was before television swallowed us whole, so movie houses, merely by dimming the lights, transported young and old far and wide, back in time or into the abyss and out again just in time to save the day. The suspense was so overpowering at times, that only by gripping the arms of the chair could one survive the moment. When the lights went back on, the audience was sufficiently reinforced by the knowledge that good had once again triumphed over evil.

"I spent a lot of time, really, in that make-believe-world that I took myself into," Max says. "It's hard to say why, but I identified all the time with the things that I saw because your mind is seeing something that is embedded somewhere in the brain. You are a product of your experiences."

John Wayne

Playhouse

3

Henry Rosenthal

Irma Rosenthal

However, Max's cinematic pursuits extended well beyond the range of what could be called ordinary because his summers as a youth were spent in La Jolla, California, on the edge of the Pacific Ocean, not far from San Diego. It was a family pilgrimage dating back to the 1920s when his grandfather Henry Rosenthal, a Kansas oilman, traveled west regularly in a failed attempt to fend off heart trouble in the tranquil seaside village with its abundant sunshine, low humidity and moderate temperatures.

A bit of a sleepy town in those days, La Jolla nonetheless offered a much more sophisticated lifestyle than anything that could be found on the prairie. The Weitzenhoffers enjoyed it to the extent that they wanted to purchase a home with an ocean view in the best neighborhood in town. Their Jewish faith had not been an impediment in Oklahoma City, but it was in La Jolla as no one would sell to the couple because of their religion. Eventually they purchased an empty lot and built a one-story brick home two blocks from the ocean, which came with its own reward as they made close friends with their neighbors, Harry and Wynn Revoir. A swimming and boxing instructor at the Naval Academy, Harry managed to instill in Max what little athletic prowess he could ever boast about by giving him intense swimming lessons in the Pacific, a mile back and forth with Harry in a rowboat and Max swimming alongside. And it was Harry who taught Max the fine points of spearfishing. "Lots of times, instead of regular spears, we used ones that were as big as tridents," Max said.

At the Beach, La Jolla, California

Max also had three close summer friends and when they weren't saddled up to a bar stool at the Putnam Drug Store soda fountain, the trio spent much of their summers on the beach, having been sent away by their mothers for the day with a packed lunch and only the bare minimum of instructions as to how they should spend their time.

Every Sunday the family, which also included Max's grandmother Irma Rosenthal, crossed the Mexican border into Tijuana, Mexico, to the Caliente Racetrack. Watching the ponies run was almost a daily staple for his mother during the summer in the States; she was a regular patron at the Del Mar Racetrack where she was often seated in the box next to Federal Bureau of Investigation Director J. Edgar Hoover, who also was a regular at the track. After the races in Tijuana, Max and his father would take in a bullfight while his mother and grandmother shopped at Milliners Department Store for silk stockings and perfume that was not available in the U.S. during World War II. Dinner was usually at Caesar's Restaurant, creator of the Caesar Salad.

"Tijuana had the second-highest paid bull ring, almost equal to Madrid. I saw Luis Miguel Dominguin and all the great bullfighters," Max said. "The spectacle of a bull fight is one of the most amazing things you can imagine, the sequined tights, the music and the horses that came out and then the matador with his spectacular cape. I saw matadors get gored, but the point is it was the theatrical spectacle that impressed me."

Playhouse

Ingrid Bergman, Angela Lansbury, and Charles Boyer in the 1945 movie Gaslight (Angel Street). *The cast also included Joseph Cotton and Dame May Whitty.*

There was still time left over for the movies, and young Max routinely took the bus alone into San Diego where he could sometimes watch four to six shows at a stretch. Life could have easily played out that way for Weitzenhoffer, as an impressionable lad with a vivid imagination could do no better than hope to ride out his youth in the saddle next to John Wayne.

But something happened along the way to change the course of events, as generally happens in life, no matter how hard one tries to make a steady climb to the top. For Max, everything changed the day Gregory Peck walked onto the stage.

In the summer of 1947, Peck was somewhere between the filming of *A Gentleman's Agreement* and *Twelve O'Clock High* when he took time off from the Hollywood movie set to perform on stage for a week at the La Jolla High School Playhouse, otherwise known as the school auditorium.

It was not something a reputable Hollywood agent would consider to be a career-enhancing move for a client on the A-list, but then La Jolla and the summer stock company became pleasant diversions for many noted actors, particularly Peck, a physically powerful but classic leading man whose work included *The Guns of Navarone, Big Country, Roman Holiday* and *To Kill a Mockingbird*. For starters, La Jolla was Peck's hometown. For another, he and fellow actors Mel Ferrer and Dorothy McGuire had founded the playhouse

Playhouse

only a few months earlier. With its launch, La Jolla became more than just a quiet getaway for the big stars of that era. It became a place to hone their craft in the company of some of the finest actors of the day.

The play Peck came to perform was called *Angel Street*. A suspense thriller, it was originally produced in the West End in London, England, under the title *Gaslight,* before becoming a hit on Broadway in 1941. *Gaslight*, or *Angel Street*, underwent several revivals over time, usually with good results.

Set in the late 1800s in London, *Angel Street* revolved around Jack Manningham's attempt to drive his wife Bella insane with his perceived kindness. Before his scheme meets fruition, a Scotland Yard Detective named Roughy (played by Peck) enters the stage and convinces Bella her husband is a maniacal criminal wanted for a murder committed years before. The play's success hung on the performance of Roughy and on this night, all eyes were on Peck.

But what was lost in the glow of that particular performance on that particular opening night at the little playhouse by the ocean was the presence of a young boy seated between his parents in the third row. "I had never been to an opening night of anything," Max allowed. "The audience was pretty dressed up but not in black tie. I was in a blue suit and tie. All of the men wore ties back then." While not obvious at the time, Max Weitzenhoffer, in effect, was making his theatrical debut, if cast only as a member of the audience. But as he learned over time as the producer of more than 20 Broadway shows, including two Tony Award winners, it is the audience that ultimately counts. It is a hard and fast rule that comes in handy, particularly now that Weitzenhoffer and his business partner Nica Burns are co-owners of the Nimax Theatres, Inc., a London-based enterprise that operates six theatres in the West End, including the famous Palace Theatre, home to *Harry Potter and the Cursed Child, Parts One and Two.*

As he sat spellbound watching Peck, Weitzenhoffer may not have appreciated the full force of the rising tension that propelled the play to its stunning climax. But he did reach a simple conclusion that has stayed with him throughout his career. "I distinctly remember that night," he says. "My lasting impression was just the magic of seeing people up there doing something that I thought was just wonderful. It wasn't the fact so much that Gregory Peck and the other performers were famous as it was the whole experience of what was happening on that stage."

Weitzenhoffer would never forsake John Wayne or the bigger-than-life characters he personified, but from that night on, Max became a captive of live theatre and a live audience. What he discovered was that there was no better place to be. There's no finer place for a showman to be, either, and little Max Weitzenhoffer was on his way to learning how to put on a show.

He started by hanging around the backstage door at the playhouse, collecting autographs and meeting movie stars. He recalls Robert Ryan talking to him all the time. "I don't remember a word of what he said to me, but I do remember that movie stars liked people in those days."

The playhouse performers headlined some of the most advanced plays of the day—plays by Bernard Shaw Scott and adaptations that came straight from Broadway. "It wasn't PG," he said. "It was whatever was current." Because the content was intended for adults, it was commonplace for Max to elbow his father in the middle of a show to ask him what a particular scene meant. "I will tell you later," was the usual response.

From 1947 to 1959, Max never missed an opening night at the playhouse, and he doesn't remember ever being disappointed. The productions ranged from *Angel Street* to *Blithe Spirit* by Noel Coward; *The Glass Menagerie* by Tennessee Williams; *Arms and the Man* by George Bernard Shaw; and *The Importance of Being Earnest* by Oscar Wilde. The performers were equal to the scripts: Andrew Prine, Wendell Corey, Fernando Lamas, Patricia Huston, Rita Moreno, James Mason, Lee Marvin, Jackie Cooper, Marjorie Lord, James Whitmore, Dorothy McGuire, Vincent Price, Laraine Day, Howard Duff, Joseph Cotton, Olivia de Havilland, David Niven, Groucho Marx, Ann Harding, Eva Gabor, Raymond Massey, Charlton Heston, John Ireland, Pat O'Brien, Eve Arden, Jean Parker, June Lockhart, and many others.

Every production during the 10-week season featured a different cast, and Max was able to see it all from up close. His own life was now beginning to unfold like a three-act play. In the first act, the stage was set with his eye-opening entry into the magical world of live theatre. In the second act, he joined Mr. Walker's drama club as a seventh grader at Casady School, a college-preparatory K-12 he attended in Oklahoma City, and dove headfirst into every facet of the theatre. "I was constantly doing things in junior high and high school, making my own crappy scenery in the dining hall at Casady but mainly doing shows all the time," he said. "I think it comes back to the point that, for me, you like to be somebody you're not." In the last play in which Max appeared in high school, he played the role of Roughy in *Angel Street* at the state drama meet. "I wish I could have channeled Gregory Peck that night, but I couldn't," he said. Nevertheless, his performance was good enough to land him a scholarship offer from the University of Kansas.

That was not the direction he was headed in life, because in the third act he reached the next level as a University of Oklahoma drama major and a summer apprentice at the playhouse in La Jolla, where he finally saw the sum of the parts. "That taught me the creative process," he explained. "You learn that this thing I'm looking at up there has so many more elements to it than you imagined. It never occurred to me until I started getting into what it takes to actually get THERE."

Although Weitzenhoffer did not totally understand it at the time, something else was planted in his brain that first night at the theatre. He calls it the "It" factor, the impossible-to-describe grip that Gregory Peck had on him and the entire audience. It wasn't about masculinity, or facial features or voice inflection. It was all about "It." And Max Weitzenhoffer has spent a lifetime in search of the "It."

"There are in show business all these theories about the "It" and how to get it and what it is," he says. "If you do not have it, you cannot get it. In movies, which is only photographic, "It" is simple. Does the camera like you? Dirk Bogarde was always, if possible, photographed from his left side.

"On the stage for me, for example, when I look at a chorus singing and dancing, there may be one performer that you cannot stop watching," he says. "It is not their singing or dancing but something in the total package."

The same can be said for musical theatre students. It does not automatically shout impending stardom for one who has the "It," but it does mean that a future removed from the chorus is very possible and their skills in acting, singing and dancing need to be added, he advised.

"However, when one has "It," they never need to be A plus," he went on. "From my years in New York, all of our auditions must originally be open calls. And I have seen many, many actors that from strictly a performance point of view are just as good as most working in Broadway shows. A cast made up of them would be adequate. But for the most part it is this oddity of personality that attracts your attention and not just stars.

"I believe that "It" lives deep inside yourself and you have it or do not. Certainly, "It" can be honed with proper mentoring, but in my brief stint as an actor, my coach from the Neighborhood Playhouse put it quite cleanly: 'Max, you will always be the hero's best friend.'"

Not all the heroes he played sidekick to were playing a part. Some were real-live heroes riding the real range. And Max Weitzenhoffer paid attention to one voice in particular.

Playhouse

The free-for-all suited some more than others, and Max Weitzenhoffer benefited greatly from the fact that he sprang from a family of risk-takers who found success where most did not.

Bertie "Weitzy" Weitzenhoffer, Max's grandfather, opened a saloon in Lexington in the Oklahoma Territory on the heels of the 1889 land run.

Alfred Drake, Max's close friend, as Curly McLain in Oklahoma!

Risk-takers

Ever since the bison stopped roaming, the middle of the country has not taken on very much significance.

"What I have found was that this state (Oklahoma) is an enigma to everyone, as no one has ever come here or wanted to be here," says Max Weitzenhoffer. "It is, I suppose, being like ET."

This was not said as a condemnation, but more as a miscalculation on the part of others. Sure, some attention was paid to the discovery of oil and the big cloud that produced the Dust Bowl. Oklahoma and Nebraska football have penetrated the national conscience over the decades. It's also true that the hit musical *Oklahoma!* still makes people burst into song, although they may not have a clue as to exactly where Oklahoma is situated among the states. The Alfred P. Murrah Federal Building bombing in Oklahoma City in 1995 did wake up the nation and brought people together for a while, but that indelible imprint was soon erased by an even more unimaginable form of evil and greater division. Tornado chasers have put us on the map, the weather map at least, with their up-close, just-in-time views of looming terror. In the end, all that seems to do is scare good people away.

That's the way it is when you are in the middle of nowhere, at least by West and East Coast measurements. The avoidable can always be avoided using a blind eye. After all, commercial airliners en route from Los Angeles to New York fly over the Heartland as fast and as high as they can, oblivious to what lies below. And the view from the East Coast is that the Hudson River, or maybe the Allegheny Mountains if they want to concede some territory, divides the two coasts with nothing in between. Likewise, those traveling by more conventional means along Interstate 40 consider Oklahoma to be a mere toehold on their slow climb to the majesty of the Rockies. On the surface there's not much reason to linger here, and it's hard to make a first impression when you're not given a second thought.

But none of the tranquility of the prairie and the unrelenting spirit of its people can be ascertained from 34,000 feet. That's also true of the innate beauty that softens a hard land. For example, there is nothing more breathtaking than the way a hillside wrapped in big bluestem grass shimmers like the sea against a red sky as light falls slowly over the Nature Conservancy's Tallgrass Prairie Preserve in the northern reaches of Osage County. The same can be said for the kind of work ethic, resiliency, and values midwesterners hold dear, which must seem foreign to the elites and awkwardly out of place in a look-at-me society.

It is not easy to glean by his manner or in his taste for modern art and architecture, but Max Weitzenhoffer is clearly cut from the same cloth. He is of the frontier and he is a proud son of pioneers. It does not matter that a rare and delicate mobile by abstract sculptor Alexander Calder hangs suspended like stars over the baby grand piano in the ceiling-to-floor glass living room of his carefully crafted Norman, Oklahoma, home. Or that he was raised in a house full of Impressionist paintings and 18th and 19th century English furniture, or that he grew up in a family that continuously drew strength from its closely held European influences. "When I was young I was always told by my grandmother that everything that was German was better than what was made by somebody else," Max recalls.

She made it sound so simple, but when it came to the history of the settlement of the Oklahoma Territory, the trains did not exactly run on time like they did in Germany. Instead, the territory was a wild and raucous place as settlers from every which way crawled all over each other looking for a new start, and Native Americans tried to cling to what they had been promised.

The free-for-all suited some more than others, and Max Weitzenhoffer benefited greatly from the fact that he sprang from a family of risk-takers who found success where most did not. Both of his grandfathers, Bertie Weitzenhoffer and Henry Rosenthal, beat the odds in their own way. Likewise, his father made his own fortune from bottom up in the oil business, going against the norm.

Bertie Weitzenhoffer immigrated from Hungary in 1885 in search of land and opportunity, which appealed to a man who had little to his name when he stepped ashore in America with his brother. But the two only got as far as St. Louis, MO, before they split up after a terrible argument over religion (Bertie was not religious, in contrast to Max's uncle) and they never spoke to each other again.

Bertie then headed south into the unknown with his wife and four children. The Unassigned Lands was the designation for land that had been ceded to the United States government by the Creek (Muskogee) and Seminole Indians following the Civil War and on which no other tribe had settled. It encompassed about two million acres in what was the heart of Indian Territory.

The character of the soil reflected far more rocks and scrubby trees than it did fertile valley, but the point was that all of it would soon be available for settlement. And what made it even more attractive was that the Santa Fe Railroad was in the process of constructing a line from Texas to Kansas to connect Texas with the rest of the country.

After that, one seismic event after another rolled off the calendar like days rather than the decades by which history usually unfolds. Nothing was ordinary or routine about the way the Oklahoma Territory became the United States' last great experiment in democracy. With the railroad came a string of land openings between 1889 and 1901 and the incorporation of

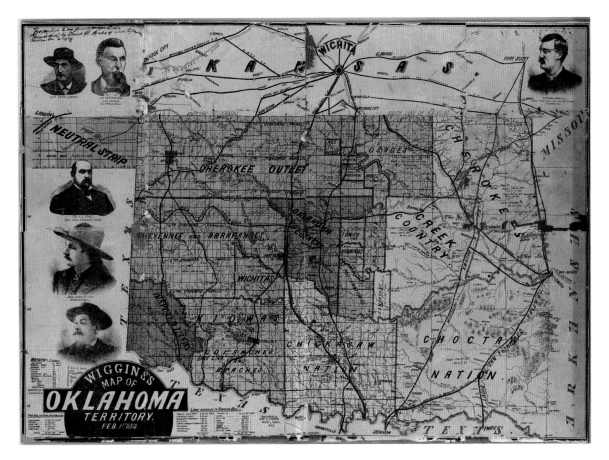

towns once tribal sovereignty was abolished by Congress with the Curtis Act of 1898.

The state of Oklahoma was spit out of a whirlwind on Nov. 16, 1907, thanks in part to some planning, lots of happenstance and faith in the American Dream. In quick order, Oklahoma greatly benefitted from the proliferation of newspapers in big and small towns; the establishment of the first territorial/state institutions, such as the University of Oklahoma, Oklahoma State University, and Central State; the importance of cotton as a cash crop; the discovery of the first commercially successful oil well near Bartlesville, Oklahoma; and the formation of all-black towns during the allotment process, all of which would have been defining events in their own right.

Bertie Weitzenhoffer somehow landed right in the middle of a good thing as the territory had no laws of its own for two years after the initial land run of 1889, and the enforcement of existing U.S. laws was spotty in many areas. This was particularly true when it came to the sale and consumption of liquor along the Canadian River, which was the dividing line between the Chickasaw Nation and the Unassigned Lands and not far from the thriving new town of Lexington, Oklahoma. And it was there that Weitzenhoffer and his partner Nathan Turk decided to open the Dutch Saloon in 1891. It

The Unassigned Lands were part of the Oklahoma Territory which included all of the lands ceded by the Five Cvilized Tribes after the Civil War and mostly used to resettle the plains tribes. The Unassigned Lands were opened to settlement by the run of 1889. Courtesy of the Oklahoma Historical Society.

Risk-takers

Bertie Weitzenhoffer was an investor in the original half-mile-long bridge across the Canadian River between Purcell and Lexington. Courtesy of the Oklahoma Historical Society, 21912.15

Risk-takers

is estimated that there was one bar for every 17 men of drinking age at the time. Somehow the Dutch Saloon outlasted all the others. It might have had something to do with what the *Purcell Register* published about Bertie in an 1893 newspaper article: "You can gamble on the fact that when there is a good time to be had 'Weitzy' is always somewhere in the neighborhood.'"

It didn't hurt, either, that Weitzy cared about others. When a part of Norman, Oklahoma, was devastated by a tornado in 1893, Weitzenhoffer made the largest single contribution of $500 to a fund supporting victims. And it has been reported that the Lexington public school system could not have operated without the tax revenue provided by the Dutch Saloon. By then, Bertie had been widowed, remarried to his first wife's sister and was now the father of six children, including a son, Aaron.

Tested entrepreneurs at this point, Bertie and Turk also saw potential in more than just what the bottom of a bottle offered when it came to resupplying their customers. In 1903, they began to bottle their own brands of whiskey at a distillery they constructed in Oklahoma City. Their big seller was "Alfalfa Bill" named for William H. Murray, a popular teacher and politician before Oklahoma statehood, who eventually became governor of the state.

In addition, Weitzenhoffer and Turk were major players in a group that raised $15,000 to form the Purcell Bridge Company which constructed the first bridge across the Canadian River between the towns of Lexington and Purcell. The bridge was a half-mile long, had toll booths on each end and was equipped with telephones to facilitate traffic. The fee was five cents each way per head for foot traffic and livestock when driven, and ten cents for a man and a horse.

Eventually, Bertie and Turk's profitable business model succumbed to the anti-saloon movement which grew stronger the closer the twin territories, identified as Oklahoma Territory and Indian Territory, moved to statehood in 1907. Their efforts to make Oklahoma "bone dry" eventually led Bertie and Turk to close their saloon prior to the granting of statehood and dispose of their entire inventory. The collapse of their business brought an end to the good times for both of them as Bertie never duplicated the success he had in the saloon business, while Turk died from an accidental gunshot wound after moving to Texas. But it had been quite a ride.

Max Weitzenhoffer's other grandfather, Henry Rosenthal, was born in Pennsylvania and grew up to be a wildcatter in every sense of the word. Widely known in oil circles as a major producer and drilling contractor, Rosenthal formed several companies over time, including the LaRobb Oil Company and Aladdin Petroleum, and operated in Oklahoma, Kansas, Texas, New Mexico and Illinois over the years. He made and lost several fortunes during his lifetime to the point that he was legendary in the Midcontinent Field where he drilled the most productive discovery well southern Illinois had seen. Henry Rosenthal always won more than he lost by a wide margin, and he always surrounded himself with fast cars and fast horses.

Standing only a couple inches above five-foot tall, to put it charitably, Rosenthal was said to be the exact image of actor Thomas John Mitchell who played Scarlett O'Hara's father, Gerald O'Hara, in the classic film *Gone with the Wind*. And his charm and benevolence could have played on the big screen, as well.

"Henry Rosenthal has helped more men in the oil game than any other individual in Wichita (Kansas)," a line from the 'Who's Who in Oil' newspaper column read at the height of Rosenthal's success. "When an operator gets hard up while drilling a test, he goes to Henry, and Henry pulls him out of the kinks…All it takes to get help from Henry is a clean reputation for fair dealing and a proposition with worthy qualities. He has been connected with more test drilling in Kansas than any other man in the state, and the name of Henry Rosenthal in any kind of an oil deal ensures its success."

Rosenthal died on May 12, 1939, only six months before Max was born. Knowing there was more oil to discover, he had become bored sitting by the sea at La Jolla waiting for his heart to mend itself, so he returned to Illinois to drill the biggest discovery well on the biggest lease the state had ever seen. He had completed 30 wells and was working on one last well when he had a fatal heart attack on a rig.

Just as his own father had been shaped by the early days of the frontier when the land was new and the liquor flowed freely, Aaron Weitzenhoffer had to learn to function with the hangover that came with the end to legalized drinking in Oklahoma. As a teenager growing up in Oklahoma City, he worked his way through Central High School selling newspaper and magazine subscriptions. Fortunately, he had a talent for sales and eventually sold his little subscription company to his good friend and classmate Harvey Everest, who went on to become one of the city's most prominent citizens.

Still unable to afford college, Aaron instead pursued a retail career in what he called "the college of hard knocks." People said he had a noble bearing, a kind expression and a certain flair. Coupled with a strong work ethic, Aaron was on his way to bigger things until a stock market plunge in 1921 and the deflationary period that followed set him back substantially.

Aaron eventually picked himself up and partnered with his brother Mark to launch Seminole Manufacturing Company which made men's pants using prison labor from the state penitentiary in McAlester, Oklahoma. It was a lucrative enterprise for several years, but much like the law had clamped down on his father's liquor business, Aaron's future radically shifted course the day President Franklin Roosevelt signed a law forbidding prison labor from competing with union labor for garment work. To survive, the company up and moved to Columbus, MS, where the overhead was cheaper.

"My father had a very interesting relationship with the penitentiary while

Aaron and Clara Weitzenhoffer and their son Max.

he was in McAlester," Max says. "When the company moved to Mississippi, my father and the warden at McAlester were still very good friends and my father got a number of convicts paroled and sent down to Columbus to work at the plant. They assimilated very well; one even became chief financial officer of the company. I don't think the people in Columbus ever knew about their past."

Aaron Weitzenhoffer's interest in giving someone a second chance didn't end there. "Years later, my father got this one prisoner paroled and gave him $100 and a ticket to California to start a new life," Max allowed. "My mother said the guy met another prisoner on the train and they got off in Amarillo, Texas, and started robbing banks. One day my father got a note from the man with a $100 bill in it saying, 'Thank you for giving me my start.' I'm pretty sure he got caught at some point. That one didn't work out, but most of them did."

Although Seminole Manufacturing remained competitive by shifting operations to Mississippi, Aaron did not make the move with the rest of the family. He chose instead to remain in Oklahoma to form the Davon Oil Company with a close friend, E.E. (Ernie) Davis, who had made a lot of money selling mules to the U.S. Army during World War I.

Risk-takers

Aaron Weitzenhoffer   Clara Weitzenhoffer

Risk-takers

20

Weitzenhoffer and Davis were a new breed of wildcatters. "My father had drilling rigs, but he was the first oilman in the state who spent more time in the office than the field," Max says. "I think he seldom went into the field, unlike my grandfather, who would use surface geology and lease property and do the things that interested him."

Fittingly, Aaron and Clara Rosenthal met in the oil field. She was driving her father around on an inspection tour of his rigs and Aaron was making a rare trip to one of his well sites. She was 17 years younger than Aaron, slim and petite and well-educated with a college degree from prestigious Wellesley College. Aaron Weitzenhoffer was a good-looking man, physically fit and well-dressed. He was not a big talker and chose to keep his political leanings and his religious preferences private.

Aaron Weitzenhoffer, who became co-chairman for Oklahoma for the National Conference of Christians and Jews at the peak of his career, did hold tight to certain beliefs. "The world needs more understanding, and I don't mean tolerance, but understanding," he once said. "People don't pay enough attention to the other fellow. The program of brotherhood is the only salvation for the world."

Everyone in the family said Max was more like his grandfather Rosenthal than he was his own father. His grandfather had eclectic taste and dove right in whenever he found something to his liking. His father, meanwhile, was financially conservative, not penny pinching, but he knew how to manage his money. Not that his grandfather spent all that he made, because when he died Henry Rosenthal left his wife a very wealthy woman.

It wasn't that Max's father was all-business. He boasted a 10-handicap on the golf course and once had the honor of playing a round of golf with President Dwight D. Eisenhower when he came to Oklahoma City. And, although he did not like to gamble, Aaron Weitzenhoffer enjoyed a good gin rummy card game at the Oklahoma City Country Club, where he often won enough to pay his monthly club dues. He also was known for his practical jokes and punchlines.

In addition, Aaron Weitzenhoffer owned a valuable stamp collection featuring mint-condition sheets of American stamps, including President Franklin Roosevelt's autographed personal collection, which Weitzenhoffer purchased at auction after the president's death. "His stamp collection never interested me," Max confessed. "My father would look at those stamps, and I'd think, 'Oh, my God, what is he doing?'"

While Max did not share many of his father's interests, he sought him out where it mattered the most and when Max thinks about his father today, he keeps referencing John Wayne. "One day Wayne was asked why he kept bringing his son Ethan with him to the movie lot," Max says. "Wayne answered, 'Because I'm not going to be around when he's older.'"

Aaron Weitzenhoffer, or "Daddy" as his son always called him, died when

Max was 20 years old and left a void that cannot be replaced. The importance of his father in his life was driven home to him on the night of the 2008 stock market crash. It was Sept. 29 and Max was lying in bed, worrying about what would come next. "Oh, my God, it was scary," he said. "I had borrowed a lot of money for the London theatres I had bought and was heavily leveraged and was afraid I would get a margin call.

"It was in the early morning and I got online and looked at the NIKKEI (the Japanese stock market), and it was collapsing. So, too, was the FTSE (Financial Times Stock Exchange). I was thinking: 'Oh, if my father was here, what would he do?'"

Then came the message: "Get out of debt."

"It was very spooky," Weitzenhoffer confessed. "I was lying in bed and I got this message and that was the message I got. I think I know who the message was from because I couldn't have gotten it on my own."

Weitzenhoffer took heed. He called his accountant that morning and ordered him to sell half of his Exxon Mobil stock as soon as the market opened to pull down his debt significantly. He slept much better the next night, but it did not clear up everything for him.

"If anybody ever asks me who I would like to spend a day with out of the past, it would be my father because I would like to know things I never got to ask him. And now I have all of these questions . . .

Risk-takers

Max and Aaron Weitzenhoffer,
Tijuana, Mexico, 1949

Risk-takers

The Santa Fe Super Chief passenger train. In the era in which I grew up, it epitomized the streamline age with its sleek lines, private cars and Vista Dome. You must remember that this was before the movie stars and everyone else traveled across country by plane. It's hard today for anyone to think that trains were magical, but they were. It was the equivalent of going to Europe on the Queen Mary.

Educating Max

Curiosity comes with being a kid. It is a given that children will automatically touch something they shouldn't and pretend they can scale breathtaking heights in their sneakers, slay dragons, and turn the block they live on into a kingdom they rule. The tough questions always come later, about the time life begins to get complicated and the consequences for stepping over the line often become painfully real. Once curiosity gives way to caution, many kids are never the same. Yet, the child in Max Weitzenhoffer did not succumb to such sinister forces and today his own rampant curiosity remains the one constant in a world he has constructed largely on the whim of an audience.

Through the power of storytelling, he had John Wayne by day, more specifically, at the matinee. At night, he listened to the *Lone Ranger* and *Gang Busters* on the radio he kept next to his pillow. Darkness can shine with the help of a little imagination, and when his father told him to turn out the lights and go to sleep, that's when the radio came on and the fun began. "You are watching something in your mind and except for what they are talking about, you have to color it all in yourself," Max explained.

For an only child who could not throw very well or make a tackle, the fictional characters substituted as a fine company of friends, given the fact that it is never easy to be the new kid on the block. Max found that out the hard way when his family moved from Oklahoma City to nearby Nichols Hills about the time he reached puberty. He could see the little league baseball field from the second story of his house in Nichols Hills, but that did not make it feel like home.

"The only organized sport in those days was baseball and when you're new nobody knows whether you are any good or not when teams are choosing up sides for a sandlot game," he said. "I got chosen early and I was so terrible…after that one time I was always the last one to get picked. And when I played for the Rattlesnakes in the Little League program, I got tired of seeing the whole infield move up on me when I came to bat because they didn't think I could hit the ball very far."

Football was no salvation, either. In fact, it added to his image problem because the University of Oklahoma football team was in the middle of a record 47-game winning streak, which increased expectations for every boy in the state who wore a football uniform. And there was no escape for Max because his senior class at Casady School consisted of only 31 students, too few to give any male a pass when it came to not suiting up for the football team.

Max was a bat boy for the Cubs spring training facility in Mesa, Arizona, 1952

"I remember I was sitting on the bench for one game. It was hot, and I was miserable when a headmaster of the school walked by and said to the football coach, 'What's the matter with him? Put him in the game.' Two plays later, the ball carrier in front of me knocked me flat and ran over me," Max remembered. "That's when I overheard the coach say to the headmaster, 'That's why we don't put him in.'"

Eventually Weitzenhoffer found his place as the manager of both the football and basketball teams, which suited him just fine and saved his body some wear and tear. And, in a touch of irony and showmanship that came to mark his theatrical career, Max's "athletic" accomplishments earned him a permanent place in school history, undeserved as it was.

He got a school letter jacket because he was the team manager and he received a school letter for being on the golf team, even though he won only one match in three years. "Because my mother never threw anything away, somehow my letter jacket and all my certificates for my sports' achievements wound up on display in the trophy case at Casady," Max offered. "I tell my son that is the biggest joke there is because if you look at the display, you would think that I was the biggest jock in school during the 1950s because my name is all over it. And it's all because my mother kept everything of mine and then donated it to the school."

Academics did not prove to be any more of a calling for Max than athletics. When he kept creating things that smelled bad with the chemistry set he got for Christmas one year, his father banned it from the house. Max was not the least bit upset because he couldn't remember chemistry formulas, anyway. And dissecting frogs in biology nauseated him. Math posed its own set of problems as Max doesn't remember ever making higher than 65 percent on a test. And he still doesn't know how he managed not to graduate last in his class at Casady. "Second from the bottom? Why couldn't I have been the bottom? That would have been even better," he says.

Max tolerated history and excelled in the drama club, but his favorite subject was lunch, where he enjoyed the back-and-forth banter between the students and faculty, who rotated among tables. Those dalliances may have been entertaining, but they did not bring a halt to the lackluster written reports that Max's teachers were serving up with his pedestrian grades. Finally, his father wrote back to them that if they didn't have anything good to say about his son, then don't say anything at all. "Once, my father, who was brilliant in math, sent my math teacher a problem to solve. Mr. Sharp, the math teacher, does the problem and sends it back to my father, but he got it wrong in the simplest way because he made an addition error," Max explained. "So, my father marks the mistake in red, sends it back to him with a note that says, 'This is what my son does.'"

Forgetting the grades, the reality is that Weitzenhoffer has always found a way to enjoy himself, even when he was picking himself up off the bottom of the pile. He used self-deprecating humor when it was called for and always seemed to be somewhere in the middle of most practical jokes that were played on and off campus. And he did not misspend the exuberance of youth on envy, jealousy or fear of failure. Instead, he enjoyed the moment, whether it was real or imaginary.

"I like to portray myself as something I'm not. I like to go someplace and become somebody that they want to see, that I'm having an amusing time being," Weitzenhoffer says. "I go to theatrical functions or some kind of other function or I go to the Players Club in New York or something where I'm with a lot of actors and people and I like to game play because they want to hear something that's not true."

Max was that way at 10 years old. He was that way on Broadway, whether he was basking in the success of *The Will Rogers Follies* or suffering through another performance of *Harold and Maude*. And he's the same today. After his father died, he was emptying his father's wallet and out poured slips of paper with corny jokes written all over them. Max's email exchanges today with his chain of close friends reflect that same — some would say sophomoric — sense of humor.

Humor is his default mechanism and it is overlaid with an exterior that exudes quiet confidence but not smugness or arrogance. It's as if Max is

privy to the punchline long before anyone else in the room has figured it out. Weitzenhoffer knows exactly who he is, not that he wants to share that information with the world. And he has converted make-believe into good box office on two continents with as much success as any product of the prairie since the consummate showman Will Rogers.

"I guess my humor ranges from Jewish stand-up comedians like Rodney Dangerfield, you know, on down to Bob Hope," he said. "In my day, everybody had sort of a sense of humor. Even the politicians were allowed to have one. Take Ronald Reagan. The key was he was always making fun of himself. Now, if you make a joke and somebody doesn't like it, they fire you."

While his father was prone to rely on the sort of slapstick embodied by exploding golf balls, Max preferred a more intricate brand of humor that was delivered under the cover of darkness and served cold. Here is the best example:

The year was 1970. Max was operating an art gallery in Manhattan and his girlfriend Fran (who later became his wife) was an art historian for the Hirshhorn Collection, which was about to be moved to the Smithsonian Museum in Washington, D.C. Fran had decided not to relocate, which gave Max the opening he needed to devise some trickery.

"Fran didn't like her boss, who was a very unpleasant woman," Max said. "About that time, I got a letter from the Republican Party asking for a contribution, which was signed by Senator Strom Thurmond of South Carolina. It came in the kind of envelope where your name appears in the cellophane window in the front."

That was the opening he needed. He took the letter and made a blank copy of it, leaving the senator's name visible at the bottom. Then he crafted his own letter to Fran's boss. "I'm paraphrasing," Max recalls, "But I think I said, 'Dear So-and-So. Before we accept your transfer to a government position, there are some questions we'd like to ask you and we would appreciate it if you would make an appointment with Senator Thurmond. You may come with or without the advice of counsel.'"

Max carefully forged Thurmond's signature, folded the letter and slid it into an envelope with the woman's name visible in the opening of the envelope. It all looked very official, which was the point.

Fran and Max both thought it was funny until a couple of days later when Fran came home and said the woman had indeed received the fraudulent letter and was in the process of being sternly questioned by her superiors as to whether she had been involved in something illegal that would arouse the suspicion of a United States Senator. "Fran said, 'Well, they took your letter to the floor of the U.S. Senate and Senator Thurmond said he didn't write it. Now it has been turned over to the U.S. postal inspector!'" Max said, astounded at how far his little deception had advanced.

The case was never solved, but inspectors eventually concluded that the letter had not been written on a government typewriter but assumed it had been written by a Republican teenager. "I considered it a success because it got a reaction," he said.

Weitzenhoffer's inherited fondness for practical jokes, coupled with his lack of academic drive in high school, likely cost him a chance to get an Ivy League education. But there was no denying that he simply had other priorities. Instead of working on a research paper during Christmas break like he should have been doing, he decided—without the okay from his parents—to install a new linoleum floor in the basement where he had created his own form of Disneyland. Every night for a week, Max trudged back up to the dinner table covered in black tar and looking for sympathy. Finally, his father went downstairs to have a look. "All he said was that I wasn't coming out of the basement until it was finished," Max recalls.

It wasn't until he stepped up on the stage that his fellow students began to really notice him. "He could act," classmate John Bozales said. "At first, we didn't have much regard for him because he was a thespian and not a jock but then he made all-state."

Max has his parents to thank for introducing him to the theatre and exposing him to the world. But neither of them tried to tilt his compass in a particular direction. More than anything else, what Aaron Weitzenhoffer did for his son was to encourage him to be as carefree as if he were blowing bubbles on the lawn on a sunny afternoon. At the same time that Max's spirit was encouraged to soar unencumbered, his father made sure his son also got a crash course in maturation, possibly because Aaron had a feeling that he would not live long enough to view the finished product.

Max also learned that his father—who was nicknamed "Silent Cal" by his mother because he was a man of few words in the same vein as President Calvin Coolidge—could only be pushed so far and that when he did have something to say, it would be wise for Max to pay attention.

While the luxury of wealth certainly played a role in Max's upbringing, his father's most notable contribution was not what he purchased for Max. It was the connection he made between money and independence, and between generosity and responsibility. The former means nothing without the latter.

"The big thing he clearly imparted on me was the fact that one should be thankful for what one has and always feel an obligation to people that don't have as much," Max says.

What he also learned from his father was that as you go through life, part of what's required is to just deal with it and not expect everyone to take care of you all the time. "You are often faced with things that most likely you got yourself into, and you have to figure out how to get yourself out of it," Max emphasized.

The lesson was imparted so subtly that he never knew what hit him. Oh, he did get the belt occasionally and had his mouth washed out with soap a few times, which was standard punishment for the day. For the most part, though, Aaron Weitzenhoffer was content to allow his son to have fun, make mistakes and learn to not fear the consequences of his actions. Given his family's wealth and yearning for privacy, Max was about as unchecked as the frontier itself.

"Kids never discussed anything with their parents in those days, but I knew I had different rules than anybody else," Max explained. "My father always said, 'If you are going to drink, go downstairs and drink. I don't want you drinking in the car. If you feel like having a drink, go downstairs and have it.' Then, suddenly, drinking didn't interest me."

The key was that from the beginning Aaron always let a little more line out over time. For example, there was the trip the family made to New Orleans, LA, to watch the University of Oklahoma football team play the University of North Carolina in the 1949 Sugar Bowl. It was important for several reasons. One, it marked the first time Max got to go on the road to see his beloved Sooners play. To him, they are really road shows more than they are football games because he is as struck with the theatrics of football as he is with Broadway.

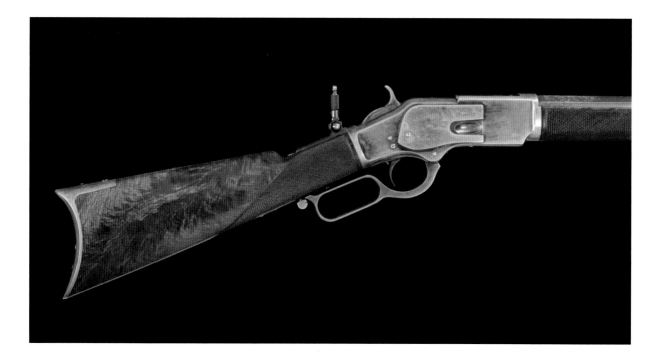

Something else significant happened that week in New Orleans. One day, while strolling with his parents through antique shops on Royal Street in the French Quarter, Max's gaze landed on a set of LePage dueling pistols and a lever-action carbine made by the Winchester Repeating Arms Company. Max left the shop with both the pistols and the rifle and by the time he was out of high school, he had amassed a vintage gun collection that rivaled any adult's.

But that wasn't even the most interesting part of the Sugar Bowl trip. That occurred the next day when his father put him on a sightseeing bus where he would be unchaperoned for the day. Granted it was a less fearful time in America, but Max was not yet 10 years of age. Plus, New Orleans was, and remains, a city of great temptation. The tour did come with a guide and Max was given $20 for lunch, which in those days would have purchased a five-course meal at Antoine's Restaurant.

"Did you have a good time?" his father asked him when he picked Max up at the end of the day.

"Yes," Max answered.

His father then wanted to know if he spent all his money.

"Uh, I don't have any left," Max reluctantly offered.

"What did you do with it?"

"Well, I wasn't really interested in lunch, and the place the bus stopped at had all these slot machines. They were fantastic, so I kept putting money in and pulling levers."

His father was miffed at the tour guide for not keeping a closer eye on his

Winchester model 1873 breech-loading cartridge rifle. Winchester Repeating Arms Company, 1873. Gift of A. Max Weitzenhoffer, National Cowboy & Western Heritage Museum. 2001.46.068.

Educating Max

Santa Fe R.R. streamliner, the "Super Chief," being serviced at the depot, Albuquerque, New Mexico. Servicing of these diesel streamliners takes five minutes. Delano, Jack, photographer. courtesy Library of Congress

only son, but Aaron Weitzenhoffer was not about to lecture Max about the evils of gambling or scold him for blowing his lunch money. If anything, he knew the excursion had been a confidence builder for his son and perhaps a bit of an eye opener. And, after all, that was what growing up was all about.

Productions, particularly those involving lights, sound and action—in this case it was the slot machines and gaming tables—have always sucked him in. "When I was young, one of the big things to do was go to the circus," Max said. "The Ringling Brothers circus came to town by train and set up somewhere by the state capitol. We would go watch the elephants put the tents up. The other thing that interested us were the side shows.

"For example, there was a woman in the circus who was born without any arms and she used to sign little bibles with her feet. I remember that not many years ago when there was an obituary in the *New York Times* about a woman who died in Los Angeles and who did a lot of charitable work of all kinds . . . I kept reading it and it said she was born without any arms and that she used to be in the Ringling Brothers show where she signed Bibles with her feet. I said, 'Oh, my God, that's the woman who signed my Bible.'"

Even when it came to autographed bibles, Weitzenhoffer has always demonstrated the passion and patience of a serious collector. It all started with the train set he was given for Christmas and grew until Max's train collection was so large that it felt like the Santa Fe Railroad had diverted its main line through the Weitzenhoffer's basement.

"The thing I learned about myself was that once I get fixated on something, I won't quit thinking about it until I've done something with it," Max said. "Sometimes, it is business related. Often, it's not. It's usually something that merely interests me. It could be something as simple as a soap product and before you know it, I will be online reading every review there is about it. I can never *not* be curious about something."

"Somebody once asked me what the best memory was I had of my father growing up or about my relationship with him," Max said. "Sure, I became fixated on trains, but that's only part of the story."

When Max was a boy, trains were not merely noisy little objects that went around and around on the floor until they eventually ran off the tracks. Max rode a lot of real trains in his youth going back and forth from Oklahoma to California, which made trains even more appealing to him.

"The fact is we had a great train in America called the 'Super Chief.' When we left Oklahoma, we took the 'Texas Chief' to Newton, KS, and then got on the 'Grand Canyon Limited' to go to California," Max remembered. "We never got to make connections with the Super Chief because it came in three or four hours later."

The Super Chief was the first diesel-powered, all-Pullman sleeping car train in America and was the flagship of the Atchison, Topeka, and Santa Fe Railway, operating from Chicago to Los Angeles from 1938 to 1971. It also claimed to be the "Train of the Stars" because of the impressive list of celebrities it carried back and forth between Chicago and Los Angeles. Max could have missed out on the Super Chief entirely because of that scheduling quirk if not for his father and the memory he made for his son.

"One day my father came up to me and said, 'Max, you're going to get to ride the Super Chief with your grandmother.' Well, that was the most fabulous thing I could have imagined. Once we were in our cabin, the conductor came up to me and said, 'Max, I have a message from the Santa Fe Railroad that you are to ride with the engineer on the Super Chief, and I am going to take you to the front of the train when we stop in La Junta (Colorado) and you will ride with him to the next stop.'"

So Max got to sit up front of the Super Chief with the engineer for the ride of his life. "I don't even remember what the engineer said to me, or if he said anything," Max recalled. "What was meaningful was that my father had arranged the whole thing. It was one of the nicest things he ever did for me. My father certainly gave me things, but it was the personal touch he demonstrated that sticks with me and has driven me to do that for my children, as well."

When he outgrew his train set, Max turned to guns, particularly those that were used to tame the American frontier. By the time he was a high school senior, Max had acquired more than 200 weapons and had devised a way to take target practice and load his own ammunition in the basement. (The collection is now on display at the National Cowboy & Western Heritage Museum in Oklahoma City.)

He became such a good shot that he could always count on picking up extra spending money from his grandmother, who gave him a dollar for every rabbit he killed in her garden.

Later in life Max pursued fast cars, sailing and art collecting with the same fervor. There was always something new over the horizon. The challenge for his father was getting Max to finish what he started before his curiosity took him somewhere else. That required both stamina and patience on his father's part because things were never still inside Max's head.

Their first showdown took place when Max was in grade school and decided that he wanted a pair of chicks and rabbits for Easter, the cute and colorful kind. For a while they were housed in the basement, and life was good. But Max had moved on to something else by the time it was discovered that the chicks were really ducks and were much too large to squirrel away down below.

The ducks moved to the backyard of the Weitzenhoffer home which was on 34th Street in Oklahoma City at the time. But that didn't ease the tension because the bigger the ducks got, the more cantankerous they became. "Finally, my father told me he was sick of those two ducks because every morning they'd get under his bedroom window and start making lots of noise," Max said. "He told me we were going to eat them if I didn't find another home for them."

Desperate, Max talked his second-grade teacher, who owned a farm, into taking them. "We loaded them in the car and took them to our place, but when we got to one stop sign, I accidentally let the ducks out of the car and had a horrible time trying to corral them," Max says.

That became the pattern: Max got the urge to do something, only to find himself in a bit of a predicament at some point and at the mercy of his father. Luckily for his son, Aaron Weitzenhoffer could distinguish between the exuberance of youth and plain ol' meanness.

Once the family moved to Nichols Hills, Max began to pal around with a couple of kids about his own age, Tom Dulaney and Bill Bonney. Nichols Hills, with its well-kept lawns and quiet streets, was not a place where a boy could get into a lot of trouble, yet Max managed to find his fair share. "We were always running around the neighborhood doing stuff," Max said. "The worst one was the best."

There happened to be an empty lot adjacent to a nearby house on the next block which seemed to hold a lot of fascination for the boys, much to the ire of the property owner who happened to live next door and who kept shooing them away. "He really got mad at us, so we decided we would get even," Max said. "We always went to the movies together and we had seen a movie where they had made a ransom note cutting out letters and sticking them on paper.

"So we sent him a note, cutting out the letters and sticking them on some paper with the message that he would never see the light of another day. We put the note in an envelope and put it in his mailbox. We thought it was funny."

A few weeks later, Max's father called him into the study. "It seems you and your friend Tom put a threatening letter in the mailbox, which is against federal law," Aaron told him. "And the FBI came to see me about it."

That prank cost Max a month of in-home detention.

Things went a little easier for him the time he failed his driving test and one mistake led to another. Max had just turned 16 years of age when he drove his grandmother's Cadillac to the state capitol, which was only a few miles away, to obtain his driver's license. The confidence he demonstrated in himself by driving there alone proved to be short-lived as Max somehow managed to flunk the driving test.

"I was given the test by a highway patrolman at the state capitol grounds near Lincoln Boulevard," he said. "We were going up a hill on Lincoln and he tells me to turn left. I did what he said, but then he proceeds to tell me that I was now going left on the wrong side of a divided road, which I had not realized. So, I had now failed my driving test and was told to come back next week."

Of course, Max still had to drive himself home and to help ease the sting of failing his driver's test, he went by way of the nearest movie house. He parallel parked his grandmother's Caddy on the street, got out, bought a ticket and sank down into a seat in front of the giant screen, happy again. But even that part of the day didn't turn out all that well, as he crashed the car into a truck while pulling out of this parking space after the movie was over.

"I immediately started thinking that this was not good," Max said.

Sizing up the fact that a farmer in overalls was behind the wheel of the truck, Max made a big miscalculation. "I told the farmer, 'This was my fault,'" he said. Then he suggested that the farmer follow him to Rudy's Body Shop where he could get the truck repaired.

"I have a California driver's license," Max said, flashing a learner's permit which carried no weight in Oklahoma. "The main thing, of course, was that I didn't want the police involved and I thought the farmer would fall for it."

A few days later Max was sitting at the breakfast table when his father casually remarked, "You know that farmer you hit wasn't as stupid as you thought he was. And that California learner's permit you pulled on him didn't work, either."

His father never told him how much he had to pay the farmer to keep things quiet. All he knew was that it was bad.

"The other problem was that I was always running into things in my car. By the time I got to college, my father told me that the only car insurance he could get for me was through Lloyd's of London."

However, leniency was not always handed out like ballots on election day. "Something else would always get my attention and I think that sometimes annoyed my father," Max said. "I also believed that when he asked me to jump, the only question was supposed to be, 'How high?'"

Max had dragged along his typewriter to La Jolla one summer when he became convinced it was not working properly. It might have had something to do with the fact that he was a lousy typist and that his fingers never seemed to connect with the keys. Max, however, placed the entire blame on faulty equipment rather than operator error.

"I kept complaining that my typing problem was related to the fact that the keys were gooey, anything other than it was because I wasn't using it properly. All of my complaining was met with silence."

Still fixated on the belief that he and only he held the key to fixing the problem, Max took the typewriter to the repair shop, where he was told there was nothing wrong with the keys themselves. "Well, my father had a fit when I got home and reminded me he had told me to leave it alone. My takeaway from that was I wasn't going to do anything he told me not to do again."

Except for the way he dressed, Aaron Weitzenhoffer was modest, even

Aaron Weitzenhoffer was an oilman and community leader.

shy. He drove a Chevrolet to work because he didn't want to appear to be better than those who worked for him, and he was heavily involved in helping others as president of the Community Chest (United Way), the Red Cross and the YMCA. "I have always felt that since the world has been good to me I naturally owe an obligation to do everything I can to help those who have not been as fortunate as I have," he said in a 1955 newspaper article. "I just can't imagine a person prospering and not wanting to share what he has. I would think he would be afraid not to share with others because the Lord has been good to him."

Two powerful forces have always been at play in Oklahoma. One came from the top down and is driven by a strong religious fervor and the belief that God will provide; the other gushes from the ground up in the form of an abundant natural resource that was more a product of dedication and sacrifice than it was the answer to a prayer.

Educating Max

Films. The "It" factor with films is easy. They can take you to unimaginable worlds and places. They can remove you from your seat in the movie theatre and make you feel like you have become part of the action.

John Wayne and Henry Fonda starred in Fort Apache, *Max's favorite film.*

Of all the gin joints in all the towns in all the world, she walks into mine."—— Rick Blaine in Casablanca

From big screen
to big gushers

More than scripture, Max Weitzenhoffer has sought meaning from screenplays and the classic lines they produce, whether they were written for Hollywood or Broadway or somewhere in between. If he can quote one memorable line, he's got a thousand in reserve. Perhaps none epitomizes plain-spoken raw feelings as well as the short sentence delivered by expatriate Rick Blaine (Humphrey Bogart) to Sam (Dooley Wilson), his piano player, in the 1942 romantic drama *Casablanca*. The events that unfolded against a backdrop of low arches, deep shadows and endless intrigue inside Rick's Café Américain gave substance to the urgency for free men everywhere to answer the call to duty in the face of Adolph Hitler's advance across Europe. "Here's looking at you, kid," were Rick's famous parting words to his lost love (Ingrid Bergman), but to Weitzenhoffer, it was the tortured lament of the saloon keeper that stuck with him, ripe with the pain of love and loss, overpowering in its simplicity and as ominous as the winds of war.

"So long, so long, you ancient pelican."

That line was spoken at the end of the 1954 film *The High and the Mighty*, and were mouthed in admiration and respect for Captain Dan Roman (John Wayne) as he walked off the runway into the mist after safely landing, against all odds, a doomed commercial aircraft carrying 17 passengers and a crew of five. The ancient pelican forevermore became a symbol of bravery and resolve to Weitzenhoffer, not to mention those who made their living in the sky.

Then there was Spencer Tracy, taking on the role of "Square John" Sand in the 1940 adventure blockbuster *Boom Town*, which also featured Clark Gable and Claudette Colbert in a search for oil that paralleled America's yearning to make its mark in the world in the early part of the 20th Century.

Sand and "Big John" McMasters (Gable) were Texas wildcatters who personified the unthinkable risks associated with sinking a pipe into the ground, often on a hunch, in hopes of striking it rich. The long odds of drilling exploration wells in unproven fields eventually bankrupted them and destroyed their relationship. But in the end it did not compromise their principles, as noted in the film's final stages when Square John rose from the witness box in defense of his ex-partner, who was facing certain prosecution for violating the Sherman Antitrust Act.

"Well, as I get it . . . McMasters is on the hook because he broke the antitrust laws. He signed up a bunch of oil operators and formed a

Ingrid Bergman

Spencer Tracy

Clark Gable

From big screen to big gushers

monopoly in restraint of trade. I know he signed them up to try to make more money, but after all he's not exactly original. A lot of us had those ideas. What he was doing, although he didn't know it, but in a way, he was working for these here United States, too. He wanted these guys to produce less oil so their wells would flow years longer and not ruin the fields. That way they would get all the oil out of the wells there was to get.

"In a way, he was for conservation. Now how can a guy be breaking the law when he's trying to save the natural resources of the country? He didn't know he was doing anything you might call noble, but being one of the best oilmen there is, he's got the right hunch about oil. He knows that it took millions of years to put it here and if we keep taking it out at the rate we're going, why, before long there won't be any oil left in the old USA. There won't be any left for him or men like him to break up into little gas stations where people can get their stuff moved around in trucks, so that you can light furnaces and homes and schoolhouses. If that time ever comes what will be the good of American schoolhouses anyway . . . Between oceans, what are you going to run your airplanes and battleships on? Tomato soup? . . . McMasters is a wildcatter. If it wasn't for automobiles, he would be driving a covered wagon. It's always been his breed that has opened up the country and made it what it is. So now I'm wondering, is it getting to be out of line for a man like him to make a million dollars in these United States with his brains and his hands? Because if it is, we better rewrite this land of opportunity stuff . . . I admit he is ornery and he's mean. He's an oilman. But he has the right idea about what to do with our oil. But he has always met his payroll and you can put his word in the bank."

Based largely on Square John's square-shooter speech, McMasters was acquitted and the two became partners on a new quest with Betsy, once the source of much of their discord, right between them. Luther Aldrich (Frank Morgan), the oilfield equipment owner they once jilted in their desperation to find oil, even supplied them with a rig, and the whole cycle would begin again.

Max Weitzenhoffer relates to *Boom Town* because there are two lessons, maybe three, to be found in Sands' plea to the court. For one, it is not a crime in America to aspire to want to get rich, particularly when you are willing to assume all the risks. But part of that bargain also means keeping your word.

Minus the romantic entanglements, *Boom Town's* storyline did not stray all that far from the heart of the matter when it came to how real-life wild-catters, Weitzenhoffer's grandfather and father among them, bet boldly on themselves in a high-stakes game of chance that, well, personifies America's ingenuity and entrepreneurial spirit about as well as anything could.

And this wasn't simply about building a better mousetrap or beating a competitor for a spot in line at the U.S. Patent Office. Just as the steam engine drove progress in the 19th Century, oil powered America's greatness in the first half of the 20th Century. The fields of the United States accounted for more than 70 percent of world oil production in 1925 and 63 percent in 1941, and U.S. oil corporations dominated the world markets from the 1920s to the 1970s. The plethora of U.S. oil also helped give rise to the country's military might and pushed America well ahead of the rest of the world when it came to industrial clout. By the 1920s, the U.S. economy was larger than the combined economies of the next six great world powers. Cheap and plentiful supplies of oil were a prerequisite for the Big Three automakers who had a tight hold on the industry for the first half of the century.

Max is convinced his father and grandfather were partly responsible for making America great and keeping the U.S. out of the hands of countries like Germany. "They risked everything they had to drill for oil. And as was alluded to in *Boom Town*, my grandfather and father always met the payroll, and you could put their word in the bank."

On top of that, Max said his father was so patriotic that if he had lived to see the Vietnam War he would have disowned his son if Max had chosen to avoid the draft by fleeing to Canada. Max clearly carries the same DNA, only he doesn't get his clothes as greasy roaming a theatre aisle as he would on a rig. "Without question, my occupation as a producer has all the attributes of the early oil industry," he acknowledged. "There is great risk with the possibility on rare occasions of great reward. I know my grandfather and my father spent a lot of nights on a drilling rig hoping and waiting, like the first nights in the theatre hoping and waiting . . . and most of the time coming up with a dry hole."

Nowhere was the hunt for crude oil either riskier or more rewarding than it was in Oklahoma where the first oil well of any consequence, which was drilled in Oklahoma City shortly after the 1889 land run, was quickly abandoned because the driller was looking for water, not oil. Based on the drilling frenzy that followed, that was probably the last time water was deemed to be more essential to survival in this oil-happy state.

In April of 1897, The Nellie Johnstone No. 1 well in Bartlesville, Oklahoma, made history as the first major discovery in what was still Indian Territory, which attracted hundreds of exploration companies to an area just south of the Kansas border that once was a favorite grazing place for buffalo and a stopover for Plains Indians and outlaws alike. In 1901, the Red Fork Gusher set off another drilling boom in Tulsa, Oklahoma, turning the town into what was described as the "Drilling Capital of the World."

Henry Rosenthal, left, was a celebrated wildcatter in his day.

From big screen to big gushers

45

Ernest W. Marland, a Pennsylvanian and a graduate of the University of Michigan law school who became the tenth governor of Oklahoma, opened the Ponca City Field in 1911 with the completion of the now famous Willie-Cries-for-War Number One oil well on sacred Ponca land. According to the Oklahoma Historical Society his strike attracted other wildcatters, and in 1917 the Garber Field was located, which proved to be one of the largest producers of high-grade crude during World War I. However, when Marland discovered the Tonkawa (or Three Sands Field) in 1921, the oil legacy of north-central Oklahoma was assured, as was Marland's place in history as one of the most flamboyant and far-sighted oilmen and politicians of that era.

Marland, however, had plenty of competition. In March of 1912, independent oilman Thomas "Dry Hole" Slick found an oil seep on the Frank Wheeler farm east of Cushing. Wheeler had paid sixty-five cents per acre for his farm in 1907, but when Slick uncovered the huge Cushing Field, the value skyrocketed. Jackson Barnett, who had been granted a 160-acre allotment in the Cushing Field, owned a farm that eventually produced oil worth $24 million. So great was Cushing's output that in 1919 its wells produced 17 percent of all oil marketed in the United States and between 1912 and 1919 produced three percent of all the world's output.

Everywhere a person looked entire towns appeared to spring out of the ground along with the oil. One was the town of Shamrock, Oklahoma, which was founded as a small farming hamlet in 1910. Three years later it consisted of two general stores, a restaurant and a population of 35 people. With the opening of the Cushing Oil Field two years later, the townsite was shifted to the southern edge of the oil field and became a boom town overnight.

Shamrock even took on an Irish flavor. Its main street was named Tipperary Road, buildings were painted green and the town acquired a Blarney Stone, along with about an additional 10,000 people. But the luck of the Irish did not prevail. Shamrock eventually gave way to bigger oil strikes across Oklahoma and improved technology that required fewer workers and the town soon faded away.

During the Roaring Twenties perhaps the greatest discovery was made at Seminole, Oklahoma. Drilling started near Wewoka, Oklahoma as early as 1902 and several fields were located in the following decades. In 1926–27 five of the state's largest discoveries were recorded—Earlsboro, Seminole City, Bowlegs, Searight, and Little River. Fifty pools were located in and around Seminole County, and between July 1926 and September 1929 those fields produced more than 250 million barrels of oil.

Seminole was followed by the huge discovery in Oklahoma City in 1928, whose centerpiece was the same field that had been abandoned in 1889. One well, the Number One McBeth, had a daily flow of 101,002 barrels of crude oil. When gas pockets were unexpectedly encountered, the result was a runaway gusher that frequently sprayed entire neighborhoods with crude before a crew could control the well.

But it was not destined for oil to spray like champagne that had just popped out of a bottle as big as an ocean. The sudden collapse of the stock market in 1929 and the rapid decline of agriculture as a driver of the economy transformed that shapely bottle into a Dust Bowl, leaving Oklahoma in worse shape than most states throughout the 1930s. Unfortunately, the new peril coincided with the opening of the giant East Texas oil field in 1930 which led to overproduction, falling oil prices and extensive layoffs. According to the Oklahoma Historical Society, joblessness in Oklahoma probably exceeded 300,000 out of an urban population of about 800,000. In rural Oklahoma, where tenant farmers made up more than 60 percent of the population, farm income fell 65 percent in the 1930s.

Because neither a tradition nor a system of public welfare existed in Oklahoma, communities were left to meet their own needs through charity and innovation. Will Rogers gave benefit performances that raised $100,000 while the Red Cross, the Salvation Army and other organizations tried to fill the void. Oklahoma City built a "Hooverville" community camp along the North Canadian River to provide shelter for the homeless who were surviving in tents, shacks and caves. Gov. William H. "Alfalfa Bill" Murray ordered Oklahoma City's St. Anthony Hospital to keep its soup lines open despite concerns that they would attract transients, and he proclaimed martial law to halt farm foreclosures and suspended oil production to boost petroleum prices.

Still, there was little that could be done to stop the ensuing exodus of destitute tenant farm families to California, and their portrayal by John Steinbeck in the novel *The Grapes of Wrath* and later by director John Ford in the 1940 film by the same name, starring Henry Fonda as Tom Joad, came to define Oklahoma as the perfect place from which to flee. However, the reality is that most Oklahomans chose to stick it out because they felt their home was worth fighting for and so was their state and their country.

Aaron and Clara Weitzenhoffer were among those determined to prove that hard times would not be their undoing. Aaron managed to keep his company afloat during the massive downturn as did Henry Rosenthal, but the couple was living in a small yellow brick house on 34th Street by the time Max was born on Oct. 30, 1939. Six months earlier, Max's grandfather had had another heart attack on a rig he was drilling in Illinois and died. The Great Depression was now losing its grip on the country. There was talk of war in Europe. Everywhere, times were changing.

From big screen to big gushers

Frontier women. There's a misconception, I believe, that *Oklahoma!* was a coming out for men in the state, that the male generation was taking over the territory and women would be relegated to the kitchen. The reality is that women have been the backbone in keeping this place running from territorial days, through The Great Depression and all the other hardships Oklahoma has endured. Take my mother. She was as tough as nails and no man could stand up to her, other than my father. She wasn't alone, either. We are still on the frontier and strong women are not the exception.

Pioneer Woman, Bryan Baker, 1930
Courtesy of the Oklahoma Historical
Society, 20699.84.30.116

For many years, this pair of Dalmatians "stood guard" at the Weitzenhoffer's home in Nichols Hills. After his mother's death, Max had them moved to his backyard in Norman.

1609 Drury Lane

The house on 1609 Drury Lane in Nichols Hills was built by Irma Rosenthal, Max's grandmother, shortly after her husband's death. A few years later, a new wing and a four-car garage with living quarters overhead were added to accommodate Aaron, Clara, their son Max, the cook and Bert Harmon, whose main job was to keep an eye on Max. Even with the expansion, it was not the stateliest home on the block, because after all, this was a residential development that had drawn its inspiration from the mansions of Beverly Hills, California. Architecturally, the 2.4-square mile enclave on the northern edge of Oklahoma City featured American, Dutch, Georgian and Federal colonials of a grand scale, along with a smattering of Cape Cods, Tutors and Greek Revivals and Spanish Villas. The lawns were expansive and well-manicured, and all manner of well-nourished plant life sprang from the red dirt underneath. About the only thing missing were the Pacific Ocean and the San Gabriel Mountain; and, of course, the Hollywood movie stars to provide more glitz and glamor.

On the outside, the house did have one distinctive touch that helped single it out in a parade of expensive custom homes that meandered along curving streets much like the Mississippi River flows. Mounted on each side of the entrance to the driveway were two iron statues of dogs, both painted white with black spots to resemble Dalmatians. That was about the only public statement Clara Weitzenhoffer ever chose to make in her life regarding her wealth, stature or personal preferences. Her position was that if you have it, that is even more reason to keep it to yourself. She made an exception for Dalmatians because she valued them more than anything else she possessed, including an extraordinary, almost priceless collection of French Impressionism art that she had zero interest in wanting to share with her neighbors, much less the world.

Dalmatians were another story entirely. They were constantly by her side. They went everywhere she went and got equal treatment to the humans in her life. Maybe even better care, in some cases, because when Clara drove Max to school, the Dalmatians sat next to her in the front seat while Max occupied the back seat, much the way a handsome pair of Dalmatians added a regal touch when they trotted alongside a nobleman's horse-drawn carriage in 18th-century Europe. And when her favorite Dalmatian Syd died, he was embalmed and buried in a child's casket in the backyard.

Max started it all, really, with his desire to have a puppy and a playmate. He is not sure why, but the dog his mother and grandmother picked out for him was a Dalmatian. Unfortunately, it caught distemper and died soon after. Undeterred, Max's grandmother researched Dalmatians some more and came up with Syd, a 3-year-old champion show dog from Massachusetts. Syd, unfortunately, did not take an instant liking to Max, which might have sent him packing had not fate intervened. "Before he went off to a company board meeting in Mississippi, my father said the dog had to sleep in his bed in the garage," Max said. "The first night it howled all night, so my mother decided the dog was unhappy and could sleep in the kitchen the second night. By the time my father came home on the third night, the dog was sleeping in the bed in my parents' bedroom and that's where he stayed forever. He was totally devoted to my mother and they were inseparable."

One night, after Syd and Clara had permanently bonded, Max came home to find his father sitting downstairs.

"What are you doing down here?" Max asked.

"I can't go up the stairs. You try it," he answered.

It seems that Clara had gone out for the evening but had left her purse in the sewing basket at the top of the stairs, which is where Syd had positioned himself, a snarl on his face. "He wouldn't let either one of us go up the stairs," Max said.

It got worse. One time at a dinner party at the house, one of the female Dalmatians knocked Max's aunt down, breaking her arm. "My aunt told my mother that when she came over again that the dog would have to be put somewhere else. My mother said, 'Well, then you're not coming over.' That was the way it was."

When Syd died from a bad case of kidney stones, an ailment that had not been diagnosed properly by his Oklahoma City veterinarian, Clara went into a state of complete collapse, and later, when Susie had a heart attack and dropped dead at the age of 15 in La Jolla, she ordered her to be put in a casket and flown to Oklahoma City to be buried with Syd.

"So, I had to call the Cook family, which operated Hahn Cook Funeral Home in Oklahoma City, and which everybody used," Max recounted. "I was talking to Lila, who didn't hear very well, and said, 'You've got to meet this plane because Susie has died, and you've got to pick the dog up and take care of it.'"

Lila then said, "Oh, my God. Your mother's dead? Your mother's dead?"

Max then set her straight: "No, it's the dog." In a way, it was the same thing.

But over time, Max and his first wife Fran grew to share his mother's adoration for Dalmatians. Pip lived for 14 years with them in New York City and when he died, Fran and Max, sure enough, wanted him flown to Oklahoma City to be buried with his mother's dogs. "They didn't embalm dogs in New York. They only froze them. So, I took Pip out to LaGuardia (airport) to air freight. I'm talking to this guy and I say, 'I've got my dog here, and he needs to go to Oklahoma City.' So, the guy says to me, 'If we

Max and Fran with Pip.

put him on Delta, he has to change planes in Atlanta.' I said I didn't want that because he could melt waiting for a change of planes. Meanwhile, a hearse drives up with a casket, and the guy in the hearse is very excited, which is why I love the guy I was talking to because he tells the guy with the casket that I've suffered a loss, too, and he's taking care of me first. Then he says to me—he must have been a dog lover—'See that plane out there? That Eastern Airlines plane is carrying U.S. mail and that plane is going to Oklahoma City, and I'm putting your dog on it now' and off he went. And Pip got picked up by the funeral parlor in Oklahoma City." That was only part of the story. At the time of Pip's death, Fran also was dying from breast cancer and before Max put Pip on a plane, she wrote him a note asking Max to bury her with Pip in the backyard when she died. "Ask your mother if that's okay," she said in the note.

True to her wishes, Max had Fran cremated after she died and had her ashes placed on top of Pip's casket and buried in the backyard on Drury Lane. "That was fine until my mother died, and I had to sell her house. Well, not many people have not only their dogs but their wife, as well, buried in the backyard, which required everything to be dug up," Max said. "Fortunately, I wasn't there when they did it because when they dug the first two dogs up, I gathered from talking to Leroy Rowland (his mother's property manager) who took care of everything, that one of the dogs looked like it had been there for just about a day. And then the casket fell apart, and it scared the hell out of the diggers. So, I had my mother's two dogs cremated and buried with my mother in her casket at Rose Hill in a mausoleum. And I had Pip cremated and buried with Fran in her urn in my backyard in Norman. The marker that has my dogs' names on it really has Fran underneath."

1609 Drury Lane

Pierre-Auguste Renoir, Roses. *Oil on canvas, 1878.*
Fred Jones Jr. Museum of Art, The University of Oklahoma,
Norman; Aaron M. and Clara Weitzenhoffer Bequest, 2000

Edouard Vuillard, Madame Hessel and Lulu in the Dining Room at the Château des Clayes. *Pastel on paper. c. 1935-38. Fred Jones Jr. Museum of Art, The University of Oklahoma, Norman; Aaron M. and Clara Weitzenhoffer Bequest, 2000*

Given the family's history with Dalmatians and backyard burials, it is not altogether surprising that Max Weitzenhoffer was literally raised in an art gallery, although unlike normal art museum patrons, he might have been able to get away with touching the merchandise. "They kept coming in, and we kept hanging them up, starting when I was about 12 years old," he recalls.

It could be the reason he has never liked to frequent museums, although he claims it is "because there is nothing for sale there." His mother hung masterpieces the way most moms put pictures of their kids on the refrigerator door. It was his normal, sort of like calling Le Louvre home. But he could only support that contention with the fact that, "We sat around the television and watched 'I Love Lucy' every Sunday night like anybody else."

It was not a persuasive argument, given that he was surrounded by more than 25 paintings and 11 works on paper by such artists as Degas, Gauguin, Monet, Pissarro, Renoir, Toulouse-Lautrec, Van Gogh, Vuillard and others. By 2001, the collection had been valued at more than $50 million. Masterpieces hung like tinsel inside the Weitzenhoffer home. Pierre-Auguste Renoir's *Roses* was at the foot of the stairs in the foyer, perfectly positioned where Clara could view it when she sat at her desk on the upstairs' landing. Claude Monet's *Riverbank at Lavacourt* held centerstage over the fireplace in the library. Not a fancier of fine art, Aaron Weitzenhoffer had surprised his

1609 Drury Lane

Claude Monet, Riverbank at
Lavacourt, *Oil on canvas, 1879.
Fred Jones Jr. Museum of Art, The
University of Oklahoma, Norman;
Aaron M. and Clara Weitzenhoffer
Bequest, 2000*

wife by purchasing it for her on a trip to New York City in 1958. It was a fine complement to the Backgammon board and table that was the other focus of the room. She wasn't that fond of Vincent van Gogh's *Portrait of Alexander Reid*, so she hid it behind the door. She had made the mistake of buying it because she thought it was a painting that would be important to own. For years, she tried to sell it to the Japanese but could never get the price she wanted, so she lived with it.

Camille Pissarro's *Shepherdess Bringing in Sheep* was another favorite of hers, but after Max Weitzenhoffer donated his mother's art collection to the University of Oklahoma Foundation after her death, the ownership of the Pissarro was the center of an international dispute; this left him frustrated and dismayed when the university agreed to share custody of the painting with an heir of a previous owner, rather than fall back on earlier court rulings that found that Clara Weitzenhoffer had legally purchased the Pissarro.

Today, her collection is on display at the Fred Jones Jr. Museum of Art on the University of Oklahoma campus along with her assortment of rare furniture from the Queen Anne and Georgian periods. As a special touch, the interior of several rooms inside the Weitzenhoffer's home were recreated in the exhibit to provide a true sense of just how unusual it would have been to consume one's cereal at breakfast every day only a few feet away from wall after wall of masterpieces.

1609 Drury Lane

The experience is a bit surreal, even for Max. "What you feel is that you are sort of being taken back in a time machine and you begin to feel a relationship with the past," he says. "For me, it also conjures up a memory, like one of those H. G. Wells' things where you're back with Jack the Ripper or something."

The remark was followed by a slight smile, but there is no denying the fact that he and his mother had a respectful but tumultuous relationship, which lacked a loving touch from either side. "What can I say, she was my mother and she gave me the freedom to grow up on my own, and she helped me with my homework. A lot of times, she even finished it."

Sentimentality was not one of Clara's hallmarks, not that hugs and kisses were a prerequisite to being a good parent in those days. But as a rule, she did not pursue a life that revolved around Max, for which her son, for his part, seemed to be grateful.

Clara Rosenthal was a well-educated woman with a collection of interesting friends and hobbies who knew exactly what she wanted. Her side of the family were all German Jews from Bavaria who settled in Philadelphia, PA, in the late 1700s. Her cousin was Nathan Leopold, who, along with his partner Richard Albert Loeb, kidnapped and murdered 14-year-old Robert Franks in Chicago in 1924 in what was publicized at the time as the crime of the century. The pair, who were alleged to have been gay lovers, reportedly committed the murder as a demonstration of their perceived intellectual superiority, which coincided with their twisted belief that they would be absolved from any responsibility because they had committed the perfect crime. Both got life sentences, instead, although Loeb was killed by another inmate in prison.

Clara attended Wellesley College, a prestigious all-female Ivy League school in Wellesley, MA, but for some reason disliked the university and most people associated with it. To that end, she would not even admit that she had been a Wellesley graduate, claiming instead to have received her bachelor's degree from Wichita State University in Wichita, KS.

Max uncovered his mother's charade by accident. "After she died, I kept getting a magazine from Wellesley, so I finally called them and told them not to send them any longer, adding that she was not even a graduate," he said. "The woman said she would look into it. "She called me back a few days later and confirmed that my mother was a graduate. I never really knew why she wouldn't acknowledge it, except I once read a letter she had written from the *Queen Mary* while she was on her honeymoon with my father, where she said the ship was filled with a lot of Wellesley-types she couldn't stand."

Max's parents married in 1938 and went to Europe on their honeymoon. He was 44 years old. She was 27 years of age and looked like someone out of a fashion magazine, a feat that did not necessarily diminish with age. Then again, her tastes were exquisite in most every regard, and she was not shy

about expressing her satisfaction, or dissatisfaction. For example, she was not enamored with France, explaining in a letter to her mother that she preferred Rome, where life functioned better.

Rome was memorable for something other than what tourists normally experience. Adolph Hitler was in town at the same time for a meeting with Mussolini, the Italian dictator. Curious, Aaron Weitzenhoffer went to hear him speak. It was a chilling encounter, especially for a Jew. "As soon as my father got back to Paris, he told my Uncle Henry that he had to get out, that this man meant serious business, that anti-Semitism was spreading and that there was going to be war," Max said.

Henry Weitzenhoffer was a man of considerable means in France, but the alarm Aaron's words had provoked led him to straightaway send his three children back to the States with Aaron and Clara when they returned from their honeymoon. As for Henry, he caught the last boat out of Marseilles before the collapse of France in 1940. He lost his printing business, his home, his tennis court—everything but his life.

Their honeymoon was a precursor of things to come because it was then that Clara learned what it meant to be told "no," perhaps for the first time in her life. "The country was just coming off the Great Depression and my father knew war was coming, yet my mother was writing her parents telling them how Aaron didn't want to buy some beautiful furs she saw and that he didn't want to go to any antique stores," Max said. "She was pretty naïve and didn't have a clue about anything. Of course that, too, changed over time."

But money, at least how much of it to spend, was always something that bubbled beneath the surface between the two. Max witnessed the tension first-hand as a small boy when, in an act of petulance, he brazenly told his mother that she only married his father for his money. She answered him with a slap to his face that sent him flying across the room. "The truth is my mother had a lot more money of her own than my father ever had," Max eventually concluded.

Beginning in 1951, Clara Weitzenhoffer made her first major acquisition in the art world, using money she had inherited from her father to purchase an oil painting by English painter Francis Wheatley. While *Harvest Dinner* was a natural pairing for her furniture, it did not excite her, so at the suggestion of New York gallery owner David B. Findlay, Clara quickly dropped English artists in favor of the French.

Little attention was paid to her purchases by Max, who as a teenager was far more interested in cars and guns, or his father, whose main artistic focus was on filming home movies with his Bell and Howell 16mm camera. As for the fine art, it unceremoniously began to regularly show up on the walls of their home via courier through Findlay. It arrived in crates and in a way the paintings never left captivity until after her death. Max summed it up by saying, "She just bought it and then I lived with it. We never talked about it at the dinner table, but I know she spent a lot of time looking at the art. She could sit in a room and it would be part of her ambiance. She wasn't sitting there and thinking, 'Oh, this is worth ten million dollars.'"

There was simply never a need on her part to impress others. Doing it her way was the only way. "Actually, my mother was pretty funny," Max acknowledges. "She drove me to school every day and, really, it got to be a joke, because she was the fastest driver I've ever been around in my life."

If the rules applied, it would have been a 10-minute drive from their home in Nichols Hills to Max's school. But rules were not written for Clara, who always led with her nose, in this case the grille of her Navy, blue Fleetwood Cadillac. Every time she came upon a four-way stop sign, she would nudge the front of the Cadillac into the intersection, confident that all the other cars would yield to her. The tactic never failed; at least it can be said that she never had a wreck.

But the neighbors sure did complain about her driving and the danger she posed. The local cops, of course, knew her on sight because she was the

Hardly anything appealed to Clara Weitzenhoffer more than a day at the track, especially California's fabled Del Mar Racetrack in the seaside city of Del Mar. Often described as a "little bit of heaven," Del Mar was born into stardom as Hollywood stars Bing Crosby and Pat O'Brien were the major forces behind its construction. Clara and her parents were in attendance when it opened on July 3, 1937. "Bing and Pat were standing by the gate," she was quoted as saying in a 1991 Sports Illustrated *article. "They gave us cotton scarves and shook hands with us." Clara sat in the same clubhouse box for 30 years and was in attendance the day Del Mar reopened after being refurbished in the early 1990s. This time California Gov. Pete Wilson was there to greet Clara when she went through the turnstiles.*

1609 Drury Lane

woman driving the big Caddy with two Dalmatians next to her in the front seat and a kid in the back. "The police in Nichols Hills would stop her and she'd start in on them about how she had not done anything wrong," Max says. "They would just write her a ticket and let it go, but that all caught up with her one day when we were returning from California."

The family was somewhere near Amarillo, Texas, when Clara got pulled over by a Texas Highway Patrolman for going about 90 mph, or as fast as her car would go. This time, Aaron Weitzenhoffer was in the front seat on the passenger side and Max was in the back with the dogs.

"I remember distinctly my father telling her not to say a word when the trooper approached the car," Max recalled. "But she rolled down the window and started in on the trooper about how she didn't do anything wrong and shouldn't be bothered."

At that point, the trooper turned to Max's father and asked him: "Can you drive?"

"Why?" his father responded.

"Because she is coming with me."

The trooper then ordered her out of the car, put her in the backseat of his patrol car and drove off, with Aaron, Max and the Dalmatians following in the Cadillac. "We get to the courthouse and my father parks the car and leaves me in it with the dogs while he goes inside," Max says. "A little later, he comes out with my mother and he's furious. But all I hear him say to her is 'You're lucky it was a woman judge.'"

Authority figures held little sway over her throughout her life. Once when she was traveling in Russia with Max and friends from Dallas, Texas, a stranger knocked on the window when the car in which they were riding stopped at an intersection. He was holding a Russian icon, traditional artwork that celebrates Russia's conversion to Orthodox Christianity. The bronze, nine-inch object was shaped like a cross. Clara wanted it at first sight, so she rolled the window down, ignoring the cold and the snow and the warning from her companions not to buy it.

"How much?" she asked the man.

"Ten dollars, American," he answered.

"Don't do it. There's something wrong here," everyone else in the car said almost in unison. "What do you want it for, anyway? It's obviously worth more than ten dollars, so how are you going to get it out of the country?

"I'm going to put it in my boot," Clara answered.

"Nooooooo."

On her way through customs at the Moscow airport, she put it in her handbag instead, which was not a good move, either.

Max remembers the rest of the story this way: "We are going through customs and the agents are looking through all the bags. One guy is cross-eyed, which makes the story even funnier."

"I want to see this bag," the agent says, pointing at her handbag.

She opens her bag and the agent reaches inside and pulls out the icon.

"What is this?" he asks.

Not fully appreciating the seriousness of her predicament, she replies: "It's my traveling icon. I never leave home without it."

No one laughed at her joke, particularly the Russian customs officials who descended on her, threatening to detain her. "What are you doing to her?" David Wolfe, who was in their party and was growing somewhat indignant at this point, then asks.

The agent now wants to know: "Are you a friend of the smuggler?"

Wolfe goes silent, but Max chimes in. "What is happening here?"

"Who are you?" the agent now wants to know.

"That's my mother," Max says, to which the agent replies, "Then you are getting on the plane and she's staying here."

No one said another word and Clara was forced to return the icon, which wasn't worth enough to be worth the risk in the first place. "My mother just thought that she could say anything she wanted to say because she didn't think these people were very serious," Max concluded. "She liked to have control, so she was always a challenge."

When it comes to women, both on a personal and professional level, that seems to be the way Weitzenhoffer has always preferred it.

Europe in the summer of 1957. That was the first time I was on my semi-own and saw all the wonders that western Europe had to offer, both from a view of history and its physical beauty, which was a fantastic experience. It created a desire in me to keep going back and doing it again. It's like the writing on a jug that someone gave me: When a man is tired of London, he is tired of life.

The Draycott Hotel, Chelsea, London

Next stop: Europe

Max Weitzenhoffer is seated near the fireplace on the top floor of the stately Draycott Hotel, thinking about Agatha Christie, whose name is on the door of his suite. It is early April and London has yet to get a grasp on spring. The morning is cool and damp; nothing new about that. Nothing surprising, either, about the fact that the city will remain socked in for another week. Yet the boy who sprang from the land of hard, cracked prairie sod and dusty cattle drives could not be more at home at this stage in life as he is half a world away on a quiet street in Chelsea in the cultural center of London, in a country whose timeless tradition and poetic nature still stirs his soul.

Max was 17 years old and fresh out of high school the first time he hailed a London cabbie. That was more than 60 years ago, a mere decade after the Allies defeated Germany to end World War II. The *S.S. United States*, the pride of the fleet, brought him here on what would be the first leg of an eye-opening 10-week summer tour of Europe with an equally privileged group of high school and college students from across the nation. Besides London, some of the stops included Vienna, Salzburg, Munich, Oslo, Stockholm, The Hague, Lucerne, Venice, Florence, Rome and Paris. Everything was first class, particularly the first impressions along the way which, in turn, altered the course of his life.

The Berlin Wall had yet to be completed when Weitzenhoffer first visited the city that was still under occupation by the U.S and its World War II allies. He took a closed train to get there, passing through railway stations where steel girders still protruded through the ceilings. In Berlin he stood on top of Hitler's bombed out bunker, contemplating what might have happened to the world if it hadn't been turned to rubble. In Europe there was no age limit on much of anything, whether it was deep thinking or drinking all night.

His mother, who had given Max a phonograph record of a World War I song titled *How Ya Gonna Keep 'em Down on the Farm (After They've Seen Paree?)* before he left that summer for Europe, was about to be proven right.

The wee hours into the early morning at the Crazy Horse Saloon in Paris were illuminating for a lad unaccustomed to being in the company of ample amounts of champagne and exposed breasts. But it was London that captured his heart and has owned it ever since. He may have grown up in a house with Scottish architectural lines and a lot of English trappings and whose kitchen was under the control of an Irish cook, but none of it was a substitute for English authenticity.

"Life just doesn't change that rapidly in London," says Weitzenhoffer. "I know that every time I walk around here, the same thing is going to be in the same spot."

He could be referring to the play *Mousetrap,* Christie's murder mystery which he saw that first summer in London and which is still playing there today. He also could easily be talking about the British Military Section at Hatchards, his favorite bookstore, or the circular tea display at the Fortnum & Mason Piccadilly Store. Or the refreshing predictability of the sole (the specialty of the house) and the attention to detail at the Ivy Club in the West End, where he is a regular. But it's not as simple as having an inviting spot to park his umbrella that makes London and the UK what it is.

"The other thing about the English is that they are more amusing," he said. "For example, there's a little pharmacy not far from the Draycott. One time I had some sort of stomach problem that I had to get a prescription for from the pharmacy. When I picked it up and read the instructions, it said something to this effect: 'Take these once a day; they do better if you take them with gin.' Well, can you imagine getting something like that from Walgreens?"

This meticulous metropolis, which is constantly moving but never seems to be in a hurry—a credit, perhaps, to the long lunches Brits seem to enjoy and their afternoon tea—embodies far more than a boy who grew up on movies, plays, musicals and the art of make-believe could ever hope to experience in the flesh. Foremost, the theatre and tradition are what brings him back to London. It is about *Hamlet,* sure. But it also is about barrel rolling at Ottery St. Mary and Jack the Ripper lurking in the fog, as well as the sight of Big Ben piercing a hole through a gloomy night. It is about the changing of the guard at Buckingham Palace, the Trooping the Colours, and the Horse Guard Parade. It is about survival and heroic figures that did not show up for work at a movie lot every day but were unscripted and real — from Lord Nelson to the Duke of Wellington to Churchill. Then, there is the country itself: "Over the years I have traveled everywhere from Wales on…they are all so mystical," Max emphasized. "You know, there are still railroad lines in this country that use steam engines, which is fantastic. Here, you can do things that relate to another era, where beautiful little country inns and country towns have been preserved."

The colorful rogues and their mom-and-pop hangouts that newspaperman Damon Runyon romanticized about have largely disappeared from the streets of Manhattan in New York City, where Weitzenhoffer flourished as an art dealer and later as a Broadway producer. They have given way to exclusive shops, super-sized stretch limos that run back and forth from Wall Street and expensive shows with outlandish management fees that take millions to produce and require a big star if there is to be any hope of breaking even. "It's hard to feel good about the creative process there," he said. "First of all, Broadway isn't Broadway anymore, and like Joe Papp, the founder of Shakespeare in the Park and the Public Theater in New York, famously warned, 'Don't monkey With Broadway.'"Today, Weitzenhoffer sees a sharp contrast between the stages in New York and London where much of what author Agatha Christie described still exists and where there is a place for aspiring playwrights, hungry actors and original ideas. Nostalgia certainly has its place, and the older we grow, the more addicted to it we become. So, at the age of 79, Weitzenhoffer could be excused for wanting to take one last sentimental journey. But that's not the principal aim. "I'm not talking about wanting to live in the past," he professed. "You can't go around dressing like Sherlock Holmes or wear a deer stalker hat or something around town. But what seems like make believe is real here."

When the curtain comes down on a performance that sprang from an artistic well, success in the theatre is ultimately linked, to put it crudely, to putting fannies in seats, and Max has been doing that with relative success since he joined the League of American Theatres and Producers in 1975. "You know, I like playing the laid-back oil magnate, but as my father told me, you never do anything to lose money," Max said. One way to do it is the way Bernard Jacobs, who was president of the Shubert Organization and Max's mentor, taught him. "Cameron Mackintosh and Andrew Lloyd Webber wanted to put the *Phantom of the Opera* in the Martin Beck Theatre and it was practically a done deal and Dick Wolf was about to save his job but at the last minute it wound up going to the Majestic, which is where it is now," Max allowed. "Well, Bernie Jacobs said it was all because he told Hal Prince, the director, that he would have a much bigger gross at the Majestic and proved it by sending a printout showing what the royalties would be at the Majestic versus the Martin Beck, which was a lot. 'Do you want more money or less money?'" Bernie asked Prince.

The point, Weitzenhoffer concluded, is that facts matter and money usually carries the day.

And as he has discovered late in life, there is more than one way to make a living in the theatre—at least there is in London. It doesn't matter if your name doesn't headline the marquee out front. What counts is if the ushers still recognize you. And Weitzenhoffer is well known in London. That's because in 2005 he and his business partner, Nica Burns, purchased four playhouses in the West End—the Apollo, Duchess, Garrick and Lyric— from Really Useful Theatres, in which Loyd-Webber had the largest stake. Today, Nimax theatres, Ltd., the partnership they formed, also owns the Vaudville and Palace theatres.

Weitzenhoffer's foray into theatre ownership began five years earlier with his purchase of the Vaudeville in what was referred to as a one-off, meaning it was an individual purchase. He did so upon the advice of his business accountant and after consulting both Burns and Keith Turner, a prominent lawyer in the entertainment industry and a close friend of Weitzenhoffer's.

Joe Papp, founder of the New York Shakespeare Festival and the Public Theater.

Next stop: Europe

The seller insisted upon retaining management of the Vaudeville for a year after its sale, an unusual demand that, nonetheless, suited Max because he needed Burns to find time to manage it and take over the booking of the theatre. Under her direction The Vaudeville became very successful on its own and that experience put the two of them in a better position to take advantage of things to come. First, they purchased the block of four playhouses from Lloyd Webber and formed Nimax, followed in 2012 by their purchase of The Palace Theatre, again from Lloyd Webber/Really Useful Theatres.

The Palace was described in the book *London Theatres* as a 'terracotta castle on a curve in Cambridge Circus' and was selected to host *Harry Potter and the Cursed Child Parts One and Two* because it is the perfect gothic, palatial, perpendicular, Victorian home for Hogwarts.

Constructed of plain London brick to correspond with the neighborhood, the Apollo was built in 1901 on newly created Shaftesbury Avenue. It was designed for musicals and named after the Greek god of the arts and leader of the muses. There are four levels of seating with three cantilevered balconies with the third-tier balcony considered to be the steepest in London, and the theatre boasts a capacity of 775 seats today.

The Lyric, built in 1888 and situated next door to the Apollo, is now the oldest theatre on Shaftesbury Avenue. With 915 seats, it has retained many of its original features and still uses water to operate its iron curtain.

The Garrick Theatre on Charing Cross Road was named for actor David Garrick and opened in 1888. It is Weitzenhoffer's favorite as he has deemed it the one theatre he would like to inhabit as a ghost, noting that it is the frequent home to comedies and that plays do not remain there long enough to get stale. "You know when you are in an empty theatre and it's dark in there with no one else there? There are things in there," he says. "There are all these things that have transpired in there somewhere in the walls or somewhere. I believe that."

The Duchess is one of the smallest venues with a proscenium arch and seats only 494, but its intimate setting makes it a warm environment for plays such as *The Play That Goes Wrong* which debuted at Apollo in December of 2015 before moving to the Duchess.

Together Weitzenhoffer and Burns also have produced more than 20 shows including *One Flew Over the Cuckoo's Nest* with Christian Slater, *A Little Night Music, Caveman, Virginia Woolf* and *Feel Good*. As a team they have received two Laurence Olivier awards, and Nimax is listed in the London Times as one of the top 100 privately managed companies in the UK. Burns and Weitzenhoffer also ranked No. 6 on the 2018 version of The Stage 100, a list of British theatre's most influential people and partnerships, further evidence of Weitzenhoffer's influence and the many talents of Burns, who was described as one of Theatreland's most ebullient characters.

The Palace Theatre, London

How an American, much less an Oklahoman, became so prominent on Shakespeare's home field is as unimaginable as what pops off the page of a J. K. Rowling novel. Ironically, the spadework for Weitzenhoffer's reverse pilgrimage—an Okie goes to Shakespeare's Stratford-upon-Avon, metaphorically speaking—and his connection to Lloyd Webber dates to the 1985 musical *Song and Dance*, directed on Broadway by Richard Maltby with lyrics by Don Black and music by Lloyd Webber. Maltby and Weitzenhoffer were friends, having worked together on *Blood Knot*, and the two joined fellow producer Jim Freyberg to form FWM Productions which invested $1 million for a one-third stake in *Song and Dance*. Both Lloyd Webber's Really Useful Company and Cameron Mackintosh, who only a few years later would go on to be described as the most influential musical producer in the world, also had one-third interest.

A hit in London, *Song and Dance* was a two-act play, the first act told entirely in song and the other in dance, and was making good money in

Next stop: Europe

previews, only to stumble badly after it got a scathing review from New York Times critic Frank Rich, who Weitzenhoffer said often panned Lloyd Webber's work. The musical's star Bernadette Peters then developed a problem with her voice and was out for three or four weeks. Although she returned and went on to win a Tony Award for Best Actress in a Musical, *Song and Dance* lost money in the end.

"I could walk down the street and see my name on the marquees of two playhouses for two shows that year," Max said. "Neither were making money, which brings you back to reality."

On the plus side, a strong friendship between Weitzenhoffer and Black grew out of their interaction during the play's rehearsal period. That led Black, who was a close collaborator of Lloyd Webber's, to extend Max and his wife Fran an invitation the following summer to the Sydmonton Festival at Webber's 5,000-acre Hampshire County estate in England. Lloyd Webber used the private gathering of individuals associated with theatre, television and film to introduce new theatrical productions to gauge their commercial potential. The weekend always included a croquet tournament on Saturday morning, followed by lunch and a black-tie dinner Saturday night. Lloyd Webber also always picked a topic for his eclectic group to debate. One year the subject was Irish tenors: Are they better than *others*? In theatrical circles, an invitation to Sydmonton was second only to knighthood.

Weitzenhoffer still did not personally know Lloyd Webber at that point. "For one thing, he is a private person and a musical genius, who like most creative people is into doing what they do," Max explained. "He doesn't come in like a volcano. He comes in more like Lawrence of Arabia."

At Sydmonton, Weitzenhoffer developed another entrée to Lloyd Webber through Keith Turner, who was Lloyd Webber's attorney at the time. Turner got his start working for Polydor Records and music and theatre producer Robert Stigwood, whose clients included Eric Clapton, Cream and the Bee Gees and whose hits included *Hair* and *Jesus Christ Superstar*, with Lloyd Webber. Weitzenhoffer and Turner, an American and a Brit, took an instant liking to one another. "It was quite clear that Max loved theatre, but his initial inquiry was where might he expect to return on his money with what was coming up," Turner says. "He likes to percolate things. He likes to get a reaction. That's what he is looking for. I think he finds it entertaining."

Toward the end of 1986, Lloyd Webber and Mackintosh were on the verge of bringing *Phantom of the Opera* to Broadway, Weitzenhoffer contacted Really Useful's chief financial officer about having a large investment in the show. Despite having a connection to Lloyd Webber through Black and Turner, Max was turned down. Seemingly, in an unmistakable act of fate, Weitzenhoffer has the dreaded Wall Street to thank for getting him back in the game because the stock market dip of 1987 changed everything. "I can't remember the exact day, but I got another call from Really Useful's CFO

Next stop: Europe

after the crash, who said that a major investor had dropped out and that they needed $500,000."

"How fast do you need it?" Weitzenhoffer asked.

"By tomorrow," was the response.

Weitzenhoffer, his New York accountant Kenneth Starr and Freydberg went together to acquire eight percent of *The Phantom*, which went on to become the longest-running show in the history of Broadway and whose profits can compensate for a lot of flops. Weitzenhoffer later invested in some other Lloyd Webber endeavors—*Aspects of Love* in 1990, the revival of *Joseph and the Amazing Technicolor Dreamcoat* in 1993 and *Sunset Boulevard* in 1993. After Lloyd Webber's divorce from Sarah Brightman and subsequent marriage to Madeleine Gurdon, the invitation list for the Sydmonton gathering was pared of many of Lloyd Webber's earlier invitees, including Weitzenhoffer. Eventually, Max and Burns, who at the time was the production manager for Really Useful Theatres and a budding producer who had been the director of the Donmar Warehouse (a non-profit theatre) were invited back to have their cast present a reading of a play they were thinking of producing.

So, there was a substantially favorable history between Weitzenhoffer and Lloyd Webber by the time the famed Englishman solicited bids for the Apollo, Duchess, Gerrick and Lyric playhouses—deemed by critics to be merely the paste jewels in Lloyd Webber's shimmering crown. In fact, Weitzenhoffer had been the underbidder when Lloyd Webber purchased the same four theatres and six others in the Stoll Moss Theatre Group for $145 million in the biggest shake-up in the theatrical community in 80 years, giving him control of one third of the West End. Other interested parties in the bidding were U.S. conglomerate SFX Entertainment, Mackintosh and Holmes à Court's son Peter, a New York theatre producer. In announcing the purchase, Lloyd Webber said he acted in order to keep West End Theatre District "in the hands that it should be kept in, and not in the hands of pen-pushers and number crunchers."

Five years later, Lloyd Webber had modified his views on theatre ownership, particularly when it came to the four straight-play Tier II theatres (Apollo, Duchess, Garrick and Lyric) which were not adding that much to the bottom line and which he decided to shed. Weitzenhoffer may have lost out in the late stages to Lloyd Webber in 2000, costing him about one million dollars in attorney and accountant fees, but this time he and Burns benefited from the same logic Lloyd Webber had used to justify his purchase. And London's theatrical community saw it the same way as Weitzenhoffer and Burns were deemed to be proper theatre people who could be expected to produce a quality artistic agenda. "That is good news for London," wrote Mark Shenton, a correspondent for *The Stage* newspaper.

Next stop: Europe

When the Palace Theatre came up for sale in 2010, Nimax was among the bidders and again Lloyd Webber favored tradition in the form of the 20-year partnership and the friendship Weitzenhoffer and Burns had forged. Furthermore, Nica was the perfect complement to Max when it came to evaluating artistic and box office potential, and she had the leadership skills, connections and experience to manage Nimax's daily operation.

Weitzenhoffer and Burns got paired up through an act of fate as much as anything else. Burns was beginning to inch her way up the ladder in the West End Theatre District when Mark Stein, a well-respected arts journalist who specialized in musicals, hinted to her that Weitzenhoffer, who was fresh off producing the Tony Award-winning *The Will Rogers Follies*, was interested in doing a show in London. Nonetheless, she was not quick to bite.

"I looked him up and I wasn't sure if this was right. I was edgy. It seemed he was way too establishment," she explained.

But Max was intent on producing a show in London and wanted to meet her for lunch. "Well, if you really want to, okay," she said, unmoved.

"We went to lunch and we sat and talked for three or four hours, a wide-ranging discussion. He talked about all the drama work that he'd done, all the Fugard plays. He had done a lot of ground-breaking work in America, and we just absolutely had the same artistic aesthetic."

With that, Weitzenhoffer proposed doing some shows with her. It was as simple as that. They picked each other out, and now they pick each other up in the way they reinforce one another. "He is totally passionate about the theatre business. He gets it, and he understands it all. Plus, Max is very smart. He may not say a lot, but when he does say something, it's usually absolutely on it," Burns said. "When he feels things aren't going the right way, Max won't rattle the cage. Instead, he prefers the gentle approach: 'Are you sure you want to do that? What about this?'" Thoughtful suggestions, rather than demands, is his style. As a result, deals require only a handshake to be sealed, and they consider Nimax to be a family and manage it according.

Besides liking most of the same things, their best assets are trust and their ability to listen to each other. Their pairing also has worked because Max got what he wanted—to be a part of the London theatre community—and Nica got to see her hard work rewarded and her place in the theatrical community permanently ensconced.

The morning of the completion of the sale of the first block of theatres from Lloyd Webber in 2005, Nica awoke to a beautiful sunrise with a heady mixture of excitement, fear and adrenaline after collecting all the money she and her husband could lay their hands on for her share of the purchase. It also was July 7—the seventh of the seven—and she felt lucky. What's more, on the front page of the *London Times* was a picture of the Union Jack along with photographs of people celebrating in Trafalgar Square. The day before London had won the bid to host the 2012 Summer Olympics. "They almost

Nica Burns, left, and Max join Andrew Lloyd Webber and his wife Madeleine Gurdon at Sydmonton.

never put the Union Jack on the front page," she thought, deeming it to be another good sign.

Later that day, Max and Nica had posed for publicity photographs and were about to be on their way to the lawyer's office to complete the paperwork when the bombs went off. London was under a terrorist attack. Four Islamic terrorists separately detonated three bombs in quick succession in the London underground train system (The Tube) across the city, followed by a fourth on a double-decker bus. Fifty-two people were killed and more than 700 injured, making it the UK's deadliest terrorist incident since the 1988 bombing of Pan Am flight 103 over Lockerbie, Scotland.

London was thrown into chaos. No one knew what was happening because all cell phone service had been interrupted except for emergency services. Everyone was nervously waiting for the next bomb to explode.

"Finally, we got to the lawyer's office, walked into the board room where all these contracts were spread out on a huge table, waiting for us to sign them," Nica said. "Suddenly, I walked out into the corridor and was kind of walking up and down, thinking about all these people I care about who were putting their trust in me. I was thinking about *Butch Cassidy and the Sundance Kid* when they leap off a cliff and Robert Redford confesses that he can't swim as they are about to hit the water."

Her fear of not being able to navigate the constantly churning rapids of the theatre business was fleeting. The papers were signed. The deal was done. The streets of London were empty as their entourage somberly proceeded to a celebration dinner at a Connaught Hotel restaurant, where the only other diners in the main dining room were there to celebrate the birthday of an aged parent, which probably could not have been rescheduled.

Is wasn't the best way to open a show. But, by that point in life, Max knew how to weather a storm.

Next stop: Europe

University of Oklahoma football. It was the binder between my father and myself. In addition, it introduced me to the art of producing a spectacle, entertainment on a grand scale. We didn't have television, so Oklahoma football was a mega-event each week that only those of us in attendance saw. That made it even more exciting and impactful for me.

Max shares a scene from Write Me a Murder *at the La Jolla Playhouse with Jim Hutton and Michael Walker, son of actor Robert Walker.*

Were you bored?

e often invent our own truths despite overwhelming evidence to the contrary. These twisted self-truths— dripping with the sweat of the oppressed—have grown like weeds over time particularly when it comes to matters of race and gender.

Even though he grew up in a family that was subjected to its own fair share of discrimination, Max Weitzenhoffer was not aware as a child to what extent he benefitted from a society founded on prejudice and exploitation. In his case, the unspoken truth was that Max was brought up by a black man, a man who took care of him and practically did everything for him, a man who could not read or write. Bert Harmon worked for the Weitzenhoffer family for more than 30 years and supporting Max was his primary role. Bert played with him when Aaron Weitzenhoffer was working, which was often the case. He stayed with him at night when Max's parents went out and he nicknamed Max "BB" for the BB gun.

They were inseparable, yet in post-World War II America they lived in parallel but unequal worlds. Bert would pick Max up from school and take him to the A&W Root Beer stand, where Max's root beer would be served in a frosty glass. Because Bert was a black man, his came in a paper cup. When Bert took Max to baseball games at Texas League Park, Bert would sit in the colored section down the right field line. Max was in the whites-only section. Even if there was nobody else in the black section, Max wasn't allowed to join Bert, or vice versa.

"I never thought of him as inferior, but I learned that under the Jim Crow laws, which were still being enforced in the South in the 1950s, he was supposed to be," Max says.

During that period, segregation remained such an unchallenged way of life in Oklahoma and other parts of the country that when Bert was diagnosed with acute appendicitis, no white doctor in Oklahoma City would operate on him. "They had their own doctors in the black part of town, but my father, who was on the board of directors at St. Anthony's Hospital, didn't want to take Bert to one of them, so he found a young white surgeon from the North who had just moved to the city and was willing to operate on a black man."

When Max was a teenager he heard stories about a large tree not far from the University of Oklahoma campus in Norman, Oklahoma, that was reportedly used to hang blacks and a few whites the vigilantes didn't like. And as recently as 1950, Oklahoma had several "sundown towns," all-white communities that refused to allow black people to remain in town after sunset, including the city of Norman. However, that was not an Oklahoma phenomenon as sundown towns were sprinkled across much of the Midwest and South.

"I couldn't figure out why things were that way for Bert and me, but I accepted the situation because that's the way it was in those days," Weitzenhoffer said.

Then came Europe and the summer of 1957 and everything about him changed—his understanding of the world, his expectations for himself, his taste for life. None of it bore fruit overnight. He was not immediately moved to find a higher calling, and he never made it to Selma, AL, and the starting line of the Civil Rights Movement, although it could be said that over time he used the theatre to bring attention to the importance of social change. Neither did Max return from Europe with a clearer picture of what he wanted to be when he grew up. His options were already limited by the fact that his grades weren't good enough to get him in his first tier of colleges: Williams College, Stanford and Yale. One reason Yale turned him down was because while his SAT score was high, his GPA (grade point average) was low, indicating he did not live up to his potential in school and was, perhaps, on the lazy side of the curve.

But Max wasn't lazy. He had a million things he wanted to do, generally all at once. Time and time again, it was a matter of completing what he started. The most embarrassing example was probably the time when he didn't get around to writing an original one-act play that was part of his drama club assignment. Either his mother wrote it for him or contracted with someone else to do the work. Sixty years later, he still doesn't want to know how it came to be. The play he was given credit for, *Blowing Away*, was a hit by classroom standards. He even got his picture in the daily newspaper. Still, it was not his finest hour. Turning to his vast movie metaphor file for an explanation, Weitzenhoffer offered this in defense: "I've said it a hundred times. It goes back to the film *The Man Who Shot Liberty Valance*. When legend becomes reality, you print the legend. Regarding that play, I didn't write that play or shoot Liberty Valance and neither did Ranse. Somebody else did. But he took credit for it his whole life and became a U.S. Senator."

The 1962 movie was a story about a lawyer in the wild west named Ranse Stoddard (James Stewart) who became famous for killing Liberty Valance, an outlaw and the town bully. In gratitude, the townspeople wanted to send Stoddard to Washington D.C. as a territory delegate. But Stoddard decided he could not be entrusted with public service because he had killed a man in a gunfight. At that point, Tom Doniphon (John Wayne), a rancher who befriended Stoddard, told him privately that he had killed Valance from an alley across the street, firing at the same time as Stoddard. Doniphon's admission gave Stoddard the justification to change his mind and pursue public office. Years later when Stoddard, who eventually became a U.S. sen-

Were you bored?

ator, returned to town for Doniphon's funeral, he confessed the secret to a reporter, saying his reputation was entirely based on a myth.

The reporter thought carefully about what he had just been told and then threw his interview notes in the fire. "This is the West, sir," he explained. "When the legend becomes fact, print the legend."

Weitzenhoffer has often deflected attention from his own accomplishments as if he were Ranse Stoddard hiding a secret and living life as a fraud. His belief that there wasn't anything exceptional about him began when he convinced himself he wasn't much of an actor or a student or an athlete, and the cycle might have gone on indefinitely if not for Europe and 1957. What Europe did for him was to open his eyes to the wonders of the world and the simple realization that he wanted a lot more of what he sampled abroad—the culture, the openness, the visual stimulation. And unlike the elusiveness of the big screen, he could touch it instead of viewing it from arms-length in the audience. Europe also made him think more seriously about something his headmaster at Casady said to Max's graduating class. He told them when they come back for their 50th class reunion and look back on their life since graduating from Casady, that the one question they should ask themselves is, "Were you bored?"

"That was the most significant comment I ever heard at a commencement address and he was right," Max emphasized. "That is the right question to ask ourselves."

The fear of boredom—coupled with having just experienced the night-life of Paris—was fresh in his mind in 1957 when it came time to enroll for the fall semester in his freshman year at the University of Oklahoma. Max was next-to-last in academic performance in a senior class at Casady that he says school administrators didn't consider to be all that great in the first place. His financial future was solid thanks to a trust fund his grandmother had established for him, but Max's path in life remained unfixed.

That's when his gaze caught sight of an interesting figure sitting near the back of the old basketball field house on the OU campus, where registration was under way. The gym reverberated with noise and energy as if someone had just made a last-second shot to win the game. Faculty representatives from the various colleges and programs on campus were sitting at their respective tables, neatly dressed and eager to sell new students on the merits of majoring in, say, accounting or archaeology. The room was thick with cigarette smoke, adding to the mystery, as Weitzenhoffer sized things up. "I was standing there thinking what the hell am I going to do? I don't want to do most of what I see."

Finally, his gaze reached the back of the room. Metaphorically it might be said that he was looking deep inside himself, because that is when he saw Professor Don Clark. He wore an orange and black Hawaiian shirt. The sign on the table where he was seated read, 'Drama.' "Everyone else was in coats and ties and there he was sitting there in this Hawaiian shirt,"Weitzenhoffer said. "I thought, 'That's it. I'm going there.'"

If Europe was the rocket that would take him beyond the stars, the University of Oklahoma drama department, along with the overall campus environment, was his launching pad. "It was there that I had the best time I have ever had in my whole life. I was learning how to do what I wanted to do, and I was loving every minute of it."

He was particularly attached to the drama school faculty where professors placed an emphasis on helping students learn a craft as opposed to making a grade. As his advisor, Clark knew that drama school required a lot of Max's time, so he always steered Max to courses that he could slog his way through without too much mental effort. In hindsight, it appears to Max that a big part of Clark's professorial role was to get him through college and into the workplace, much like Max's own father had guided him through the wilderness of adolescence. "After Mr. Clark died, I got a letter from his wife after I won a Tony Award saying how proud he would have been of me," he said with pride.

"Hands-on" would be a good way to describe the focus of the drama school. And if he was nothing else, Max was always an eager participant who quickly became immersed in every aspect of putting on a show from building scenery and sets to serving on the stage crew, costume crew and lighting crew. "I think we had the most productions of one-act plays in school history as well as graduate and regular productions. There were so few of us that everybody was involved in every aspect constantly."

Originally, Max wanted to be a scene designer. The reality was that he was a terrible one. He was not a talented draftsman and he lacked the natural drawing talent. He was allowed to design a couple of shows, but if he had not been secretly helped by Ray Larsen, the head of the design department who would come in and clean up Max's mistakes, the show would have been a disaster.

He also had no interest or perceived talent in costume design. Lighting was okay, but just okay. "Basically, I was only good at all-around knowing stuff and what to do. And I was good at stage managing," Weitzenhoffer offered.

A stage manager has the taxing role of making sure everything moves along exactly as called for by the script. This requires some technical and lighting knowledge as well the ability to oversee everything from the time the curtain goes up until it goes down. Stage managers can have a good career on Broadway where they oversee rehearsal and manage the actors and the production, and by the time he left the University of Oklahoma, Weitzenhoffer had an extensive list of credits as a stage manager.

He sharpened his skills every summer by returning to La Jolla and the playhouse where he started out as a 20-hour-per-week apprentice, mostly performing grunt work. All in all, it was a heady time as the other apprentices included children of actors Michael Walker, Macdonald Carey, Ethel Merman, and Dan Duryea, who recognized it was a good place for their children to learn about the craft.

The next summer Max was put in charge of the apprentice program and by the third year he was directing children's shows and supervising all the other apprentices. From there, he was named company manager by the new producer of the Playhouse, Ruth Burch, who was also the casting director for Desi Lou Productions.

"That's where I really learned on the job," Max said.

The defining moment came one day in a two-hour timespan between the matinee and evening performance of a play starring Jack Weston. "The No. 2 woman in the show decided she would try to commit suicide in her dressing room. I think she took a bunch of pills, after which she passed out and had to be taken away," Max recalled.

With the clock ticking on raising the curtain on the evening performance, Weitzenhoffer decided to put one of the apprentices on stage for her with a book so that she could read the part. There was no other way to save the show in his mind. At that point, Weston declared he wouldn't go on stage with an apprentice. "I called Ruth in Los Angeles and said, 'What in the hell do I do now?' She said, 'He's under contract. Order him to go on stage.'"

Weitzenhoffer was 20 years old and green. In contrast, Weston was as intimidating in person as some of the characters he played on the stage and on film, and he had a long list of credits to his name. "So, I go into his dressing room and he's a complete sonofabitch," Max said. "I tell him that if he doesn't go on stage, I will put him up on charges (with Actor's Equity). He does a lot of screaming at me, but he does the show and we got through it."

The next time Ruth showed up she gave Max some advice that stayed with him. "One thing you must learn if you are going to be the company's business manager is you have to learn what everybody does, and you have to learn that it's not your job to do their job because your job is overseeing everything. If somebody isn't doing their job, you don't do it for them. You get the person who's supposed to be doing it to do it. Otherwise, you will never be able to function in this business."

Weston personified the temperamental actor to a tee, but Weitzenhoffer eventually came to realize that it was not wise to typecast every actor who headlined a show as a prima donna. Once, Weitzenhoffer was in New York to see *Wicked* starring Joel Gray and Kristen Chenoweth when in the middle of the first act the scenery broke down, meaning all the moving pieces stopped working and the scenery had to be repaired. "I thought it was really cool because rather than everybody sitting in the audience and waiting and waiting, Gray comes out and starts entertaining us," Weitzenhoffer recalls. "Actors' personalities generally mirror society as a whole."

Were you bored?

81

Over the years Weitzenhoffer happened to do a lot of business with director Mike Nichols who was famous for directing the Academy Award-winning film *Who's Afraid of Virginia Woolf* and *Barefoot in the Park* on Broadway. One day Nichols, who at the time was filming the 1994 movie *Wolf* with Jack Nicholson and Michelle Pfeiffer on location in Long Island, NY, asked Max if he wanted to be an extra in the film. "It's a great story," Nichols recalled. Weitzenhoffer admitted that it sounded like fun, so he joined the extras' pool to see for himself.

"They're shooting all night, every night out on Long Island, and it's two big party scenes," Max says. "One is a dinner scene, and it's so cold out there that we all have to wear thermal underwear because of the conditions at night. I knew then that movie-making is hard.

"For another thing, continuity is the major thing; like, we had to be photographed the first thing before the party scene and every night before they did the same scene you had to make sure the photograph matched every part of your costume exactly as the original photograph."

But the cold and the repetition were not the major impediments. That honor fell to actor Jack Nicholson, who kept 200 people waiting until midnight to start shooting so that he could watch the Los Angeles Lakers basketball games in his trailer. Nicholson, obviously, was too big of a Laker fan for the cast and crew's personal comfort.

Weitzenhoffer was already a two-time Tony Award-winning producer at that point, but none of the other extras had a clue who he was until after five takes of a scene where Max had to keep getting up from a table, going out and coming back into the room. Nichols finally screamed at him, "Hey, Max, how would you like to be so hard up that you have to do this for a living?"

At that point Max was getting looks from 50 to 60 extras, and the stares only intensified. "We have a scene with a cocktail party and we're put in groups. Then the camera comes through the middle of each group," Max offered. "One has Nicholson and some extras; one has Christopher Plummer in it; the other has me and some other extras. So, they do this thing and Nichols comes up to me and says, 'Okay, Max, when the camera gets here I want you to say this' and he gives me a line. At that point, I got killer looks from the other extras because now I have a speaking part, which means I got a pay upgrade—$2,500 plus residuals. And I became eligible to be a member of Screen Actors Guild."

The next night the assistant director cast Max in another scene where he was supposed to catch the camera out of the corner of his eye, say his line and step out of the way. Almost immediately, Max hears "cut," followed by a gesture from the assistant director to come with him.

"He tells me that it looks like I was falling over backwards after I said my line," Max said. "He then asked me why I couldn't do it like Christopher Plummer?"

Were you bored?

Weitzenhoffer wound up on the cutting room floor, which was indicative of his acting career in general. His performance in *Gas Light* (the play that kept following him around as a youth) at Casady was worthy enough to earn him a scholarship offer to the University of Kansas, yet that was a mirage, too.

While he was always serviceable on stage in college, the preparation required to get him there was nothing short of an ordeal. Before every performance in which he was ever cast, he was never sure he would remember his lines. "The night before, I'd fill the bathtub up with warm water and I would get in and go through everything in my head," he said. "And that's why I wasn't a good actor. I wasn't natural."

The full realization that he was not cut out for acting came to him one summer in La Jolla when he had a part in Gore Vidal's *Best Man*, a play about two political candidates vying for their party's presidential nomination. Weitzenhoffer had multiple roles in the play, ranging from being a member of the Texas delegation to an inquiring reporter. At one performance his mind was on something else and he forgot to deliver his line. "I thought, 'Oh, shit' because I expected the stage manager to come up to me and start yelling at me, but nobody said anything. And that's when I decided this was a waste of time because nobody cared that I didn't say the only line I had."

One of his other favorite drama professors, Rupel Jones, said that acting is listening and reacting. "It sounded simple-minded but it's not," Max commented. "You listen to what somebody's telling you, what the other actor is telling you, and your lines are the reaction to what you've heard from him or her. It's not about waiting for him to stop and then saying your lines. It's not thinking to yourself 'Oh, he's saying this so now I have to say that.'"

Weitzenhoffer's take was that the key to acting was not overthinking the situation. It was not a good match for a young man who was geared to thinking too much on stage, which was in stark contrast with his off-stage demeanor. Confirmation that he was indeed a technical drama major and not an actor came the semester he took Mr. Jones' acting course.

"We were doing a scene from *Mr. Roberts* in the studio theatre when Mr. Jones comes up to me and two of my friends and says to us, 'You look like you are sleep walking out there.'" Their solution was to stash a bottle of whiskey behind the fireplace that was part of the set and take a big swig before going out on stage to do a scene. "At some point, Mr. Jones said to us, 'I don't know what you are doing, but it is a big improvement.'"

Nothing, of course, remains a secret forever, and at the end of the semester, Jones called for the class to gather around him and then he put it all on the table. "I just want to let you know that there are some of you who think you need artificial stimulates to get through this class, but it's not true." And then he laughed.

When it came to Max, Jones and the entire drama school faculty had the

Were you bored?

same teaching style as his father: Don't give him false hope. Let curiosity rule the day, and he might turn out to be somebody who actually makes a living in the theatre.

"It took me years to be on a first-name basis with Mr. Jones, who had come from Harvard," Max said. "After he died, his wife told me that I was one of his favorite students because I had the personality that when I made up my mind for what I wanted, I would never let up and that I had a personality that kept it going from there."

As highly as he may have been thought of by Jones, Weitzenhoffer was never cast for a major role in any of the plays Jones produced. After one of his rejections, Max went to him in desperation: "Look, there are these parts for spear holders…what about that?"

The reply was curt: "You are too short."

The point was Jones had the ability to recognize who was likely to make it as an actor and who wasn't. And the students with the most acting potential continually got the best parts rather than running what Weitzenhoffer calls a "love nest" where everyone gets to pad their résumé by getting a lead role, whether they deserve it or not. In his case, Jones envisioned a different path for Max—production. It was not flashy, but it ultimately paid off.

Weitzenhoffer's maturation also was heavily influenced by a nutritious learning environment as cultivated by OU president Dr. George Lynn Cross, a fatherly figure who is regarded as one of the leading educators in Oklahoma history. As president from 1943 to 1968, Cross presided over a remarkable time of enrichment in the university's history, beginning with the return of World War II veterans to campus who were eager to take advantage of the GI Bill and culminating with the slow demise of segregation and the rise of the Civil Rights Movement. In between, he oversaw the construction of 37 new buildings, a massive growth in land mass and the remarkable achievements of the football team under Coach Bud Wilkinson in the form of an unprecedented 47-game winning streak between 1947 and 1953.

Cross was trained as a botanist, had a quick wit and was beloved by both students and faculty. His most famous quote came out of a tense budget meeting with tight-fisted state legislators. After being grilled for almost an hour about why he believed the university needed more money, a frustrated Cross reportedly said, "I would like to build a university of which the football team can be proud."

The University of Oklahoma is also where Max met some friends for life, especially Larry Wade, who became his roommate and later served alongside Max as a university regent. Weitzenhoffer and Wade were members of Delta Kappa Epsilon whose fraternity house was located at the main entrance to campus. Normally the DKEs liked attention, but in one case it could have proved costly if not for Cross.

It was the 1957 Homecoming and the University of Oklahoma had a big

Dr. George Lynn Cross

Were you bored?

game coming up against Notre Dame University. The Sooners were riding a 47-game winning streak. In fact, the last time they had been defeated came in the opening game of 1953 when Notre Dame won, 28-21. In 1956, Oklahoma had blasted Notre Dame, 40-0 in South Bend, IN. Coming into the '57 game, Sports Illustrated slapped Sooners' running back Clendon Thomas on its cover under the headline, "Why Oklahoma Is Unbeatable." Such high praise for the Sooners made perfect sense as the Sooners were already winners of seven straight games that season, while Notre Dame was fresh from two consecutive losses.

The OU campus was primed for another victory, especially the DKEs, who decorated their front lawn with a giant Notre Dame football player made of paper-mâché, wood and chicken wire. The Fighting Irish caricature was halfway on his back with his legs stretched limply all the way across the lawn. Nonetheless, he was so big that the top of his helmet reached the second floor as he sat dazed on the ground. He had been knocked down by the Sooners' invincibility, and it was obvious he wasn't getting up. Now this was not exactly the age of special effects, but thanks to the ingenuity of some Korean War veterans in the fraternity who had engineering experience, the player's arm moved up and down while a rocket on a high wire zoomed across the yard and a recorded voice blared out, "What hit me? Arrows, atoms or the Big Red?" 'Arrows and Atoms' was the theme of Homecoming while the Sooners were known as Big Red. It was quite a novelty, without a doubt.

Were you bored?

(TOP) *Max cuts the ribbon at the opening of the opening of the A. Max Weitzenhoffer Performing Arts Theatre, named for his father, on the University of Oklahoma campus.*

(BOTTOM) *Max, Ayako, Nikki and Owen at the opening of the Aaron M. and Clara Weitzenhoffer Collection at the Fred Jones Jr. Museum of Art on the OU campus.*

When you win all the time, losing has no meaning. The brain refuses to process it and the heart, well, the heart is so taken with winning that it would never look at another emotion, particularly a losing one. Therefore, that rainy Saturday, Nov. 16, 1957, was heartbreaking for Sooner fans everywhere after Notre Dame scored a touchdown in the final minutes on a fourth-down play from the three-yard line to shut out Oklahoma, 7-0, ending Oklahoma's record winning streak.

It was especially tough on the DKEs who demonstrated their deep sense of loss by refusing to remove the paper-mâché giant from their lawn so that they could sit on their porch and pelt it with empty beer cans. The rains came again and the paper-mâché started withering away as the empty beer cans multiplied. Finally, the DKEs got a phone call from the president's office: "President Cross would appreciate it if you would take it down and remove the beer cans."

He didn't send in the troops or make demands. He gave everyone a little time to heal. That was the way Dr. Cross ran the university. After all, he understood the DKE mindset, as well as that of most of his students. The next year, the DKE fraternity had to appear before the Dean of Students and Dr. Cross where the dean went on a rampage much like the dean in the film *Animal House*. Finally, he was interrupted by Dr. Cross, who said, "Weren't you ever young once?"

Since his graduation, Weitzenhoffer has given more than $60 million in total to the university. In addition to the paintings, he donated $5 million to start the musical theatre program at OU and has contributed several other millions of dollars over the years to support scholarships for drama students and athletes. All of it has been individual giving and not through the auspices of a foundation. He also has donated his time as an adjunct faculty member and as a 14-year member of the board of regents.

It is payback of the highest order. "There is, for my part, a truth," he says. "My giving has always been based on the Cross years. I owe a great deal of gratitude to Dr. Cross and the faculty, especially to Rupel Jones and Don Clark—not to forget Bud and football. I was mentored by real professionals in the theatre."

Ironically, Max finally did land the one big part he was seeking at the end of his junior year when Jones invited him to join the cast that was going on a USO tour to put on plays for troops in the Far East. Before he was scheduled to leave, he went home at Thanksgiving to tell his parents. His father, who was having what had been diagnosed two years earlier as sciatic back trouble, had just returned from the Mayo Clinic. Max was told his father had cancer and his liver and kidneys were failing. His father was dying. Max resigned from the show. An actor he wasn't meant to be. Something else would pop up. It always did.

Were you bored?

Kandinsky. He wrote that the "It" factor with art is that when you look at a work of art you are in direct communication with the artist, maybe over centuries or decades of time. But if the piece of art really works for you, that connection is bridging the gap in time because the artist is literally speaking to you by putting something of his own personality and emotion into that work and you either are moved or you're not.

Wassily Kandinsky, A Few Points. *Oil on board, 1925*

This painting of Col. Owen Thursday was used in the film Fort Apache. *Max Weitzenhoffer purchased it years later because the film had inspired him to name his son Owen.*

Kandinsky had it right

Before Max's father died he warned Max against going to Hollywood, that the big screen was a false god, manipulated by men who might not keep their word; whereas Broadway had Oscar Hammerstein and Richard Rodgers, people you could trust. It was probably the closest his father ever came to giving his son a direct order. But when you grow up under the influence of *Fort Apache*, *Stagecoach* and *She Wore A Yellow Ribbon*, among others, how could a young man not want to go west?

Max hated horses but he always loved the cavalry, so much so that years later he named his only son Owen after Lt. Colonel Owen Thursday, the commanding cavalry officer in *Fort Apache*. The film was his favorite western of them all, primarily because he liked the plot. "*She Wore A Yellow Ribbon* is really about a retiring army officer who spent his whole life in the army, and, just like that, it was all over for him," Max explained. "*Fort Apache* is much more complicated because it's about a commanding officer who is assigned to a remote outpost in the West. It's really based on George Custer, who'd been a general and then reduced in rank after the Civil War and wound up on a post where the land wasn't worth fighting for and the troops were sloppy.

John Wayne as Captain Kirby York in Fort Apache.

"Then he was a Martinet and he basically knows everything, but doesn't really know very much and then at the end, he insults the Indians. He thinks he can take them on, and then he gets himself and his whole command killed. It's the same as the Custer story.

For some perspective, Max had been suddenly thrust into his own personal outpost in life, much like Colonel Thursday, who didn't know the first thing about the frontier or fighting Indians. Weitzenhoffer could relate. He was 21 years old and with his father's death, he no longer had anyone to run interference for him when it came to his very formidable mother. And he certainly wasn't sold on being an actor or anything else, for that matter. Seeing Europe had opened his eyes as to what life had to offer, but he wasn't exactly sure which bus to hop on for the trip.

He finally concluded the only thing to do was walk into the student union on the OU campus and join the U.S. Navy. He didn't exactly fit the profile of a military man, although several family members had served in the Spanish American War and World War I. But he could sail a small sailboat, at least. And he knew he didn't want to be drafted, which was a strong possibility in 1961 for men whose college deferment had expired. "What do I do?" he thought. "So then I started getting a lot of instructions from my friends who had been drafted: Become a chaplain's assistant, one said. Or volunteer for gardening work, at which point you spend most of your time watering officers' lawns for two years. Or if you become an officer, try to get yourself appointed to be an aide."

None of that appealed to Max, so he stepped up to the U.S. Navy recruiter's booth with a purpose, having concluded it would be a far better move than getting drafted. The recruiter promptly told him to sit down and take a test. "I remember one section of it involved a lot of pulleys and wheels and I had to decide if one pulley went one way, which way would the other one go. I had no clue."

In an upset, Max somehow passed by a single point but then flunked the physical based on his medical history. "They asked for reports from my family doctor, which showed that two years earlier I had been treated for a nervous stomach or an ulcer and they turned me down based on that," he allowed.

A month later, sure enough, he got his draft notice and was filling out the paperwork at the enlistment office when he got to a line that read: "Have you ever been rejected for military service?"

Well, yes, that was the case, and because he had flunked his U.S. Navy physical, Weitzenhoffer got classified 1Y, which meant he only would be called into service in the event of war or national emergency. Vietnam had yet to sink into the bloody quagmire it became, and by the time it did, Max was considered too old to fight in Southeast Asia (and possibly die).

That put him back at loose ends. On a lark, he went to Austria for a few months to learn to ski. Then he volunteered to work in Republican Henry Bellman's successful Oklahoma gubernatorial race, calling it a privilege to get to know and campaign alongside one of Oklahoma's most popular statesmen. He took an around-the-world trip with a friend and even went to Mississippi with the thought of becoming involved in the family garment business. He was not meant to be a son of the south, either.

"I went down there to look around after my father died and came back and thought that I should try this for a summer," Max offered. "I always liked fast cars, so at the time I was driving a Mercedes 300SL roadster, and my uncle sent word back that if I came down to work in the company I wasn't allowed to bring my car because it wouldn't look good in the parking lot. I could deal with a lot, but this was a side of me that wasn't moveable. So, later my cousin went to work for the company and committed suicide. That's how bad it was for him. We had management that had been there forever."

Although it appeared his priorities were badly misplaced, Weitzenhoffer's resolve paid off in the end. When the company was floundering in 1991, Max spun off the manufacturing piece and moved the apparel operation to Kalamazoo, Michigan. Today, the Edwards Garment Company has more

Kandinsky had it right

than 200 employees with annual sales of more than $80 million and is an industry leader in the production of career apparel. Weitzenhoffer credits the company's success to a talented and dedicated management team and a skilled workforce, but Edwards also personifies his business acumen when it comes to both the calculated risks he is willing to take and the people with whom he surrounds himself.

Eventually Weitzenhoffer took the advice of friends who kept urging him to go to Los Angeles. Really, it's surprising it took as long as it did for him to make his way to Hollywood. In 1961, a family friend had arranged for him to attend the Academy Awards show and, for a moment, it was like Paris all over again.

"This is burned in my memory bank as if it happened yesterday," Max said. "It was the year *Ben Hur* won Best Picture and afterward there was a party and a big sit-down dinner. Elizabeth Taylor arrived with Eddie Fisher. She had on a yellow dress, and I can tell you that she was the most beautiful person I have ever seen in my whole life. She was at the top of the stairs. All I could think was, 'Wow, now, she looks like a movie star.' I'm immune to movie stars now, but one reason is they don't look like that anymore."

He has met more celebrities than he can count in his career, but there is only one he would put in the same category with Elizabeth Taylor. When Max was in the early stages of producing *Harold and Maude*, he flew to London with agent Kay Brown, who represented Colin Higgins, the author of the play. She also had been a classmate of Max's mother at Wellesley and, more notably, was the one who brought Margaret Mitchell's novel *Gone with the Wind* to the attention of movie mogul David O. Selznick, for whom she worked in 1936. "Kay said to me on the plane, 'A friend of mine is picking me up, do you want a ride with us from the airport?'

Their chauffeur so happened to be actress Ingrid Bergman. "In the car, she started asking questions about some show I was talking about, *A Day in Hollywood/A Night in the Ukraine,* and she said that she would like to see it. I asked her if I could take her, and she agreed. I went over to pick her up and, boy, was that something. We had drinks and dinner and then we went to the theatre. It was all very nice. And I still haven't torn her phone number and address out of my old address book. Never, ever will. I'm just like everybody else."

While he has celebrity crushes, Weitzenhoffer also has had the luxury of maintaining celebrity status. For one thing, when he finally went job hunting in Hollywood, he didn't have to hitchhike and wait tables until he was discovered as tradition calls for. His family knew people in Hollywood who knew other people, which meant he could at least get past the reception desk. Still, it did not go well.

The initial interview lined up for him was with an executive at Universal Studios who was looking for an assistant. "I went into his paneled office and

Kandinsky had it right

Humphrey Bogart with Lauren Bacall and Marilyn Monroe
at the peak of the Golden Age of Hollywood.

the first thing I see are two little dogs running at me with pink ribbons in their hair," Max said. "The next thing I remember is he's talking to me and he's got his hands on my shoulders. I thought, well, this is not exactly my idea of a job; he's looking for something else."

Max's next interview was with Gordon Sawyer, the sound director at Samuel Goldwyn Productions, who won three Oscars for his work and was nominated 13 other times. "They were scoring *Porgy and Bess*, and I knew it wasn't for me because there was just a mass of machines with dials going up and down. I was totally lost."

Next on the list was John Wayne's Batjack Productions. Unfortunately, Batjack had just finished filming *The Alamo* and was out of money, so it wasn't hiring. It was too bad for Max because it was the one place in Hollywood that appealed to him, which was not exactly a surprise given its connection to John Wayne.

Robert Mitchum

A friend of his from Los Angeles gave him something else to think about as Max paraded from interview to interview. He kept assuring him he would find a job. But he also warned him that once he got one, Max would spend every evening looking for another one because nobody keeps their job for long in Hollywood.

Believing that to be true, Weitzenhoffer went home and took a job in public relations with the state health department in Oklahoma City. It was a long way from Hollywood and not far from the nearest dead end. It appeared he was going in the opposite direction from Europe and the life he envisioned as a teenager in Paris.

It was not an accident, but somehow Max wound up one day at his mother's house in Nichols Hills engaged in conversation with his mother's art dealer. David Findlay owned a high-end art gallery on 57th Street in Manhattan. Not only did he introduce Clara Weitzenhoffer to French Impressionism, he also became her new companion.

Gary Cooper

But on this day Findlay had his eye on Max. "Why don't you come to New York and work for me—work in the gallery?" said Findlay, whose family had been in the art business since 1870 and had recently opened his Manhattan gallery.

The thought of one day selling the kind of pictures his mother had hanging in the living room had never crossed his mind as a teenager. He had never even had one serious conversation about art with his mother. All he knew was that price had very little to do with what she liked. "We had a Picasso in the house one time, and she hated it," he said. "I rather liked it, but she couldn't wait to send it back."

What he did know about himself was that he was a product of his own experiences, or soon would be. "Your mind is seeing something that is embedded somewhere in the brain. It will come out later. I relied a lot on visual stimulation, movies, theatre," he offered. "Art is different. It is certainly

Errol Flynn

visual, but Wassily Kandinsky (a Russian painter and theorist credited for painting the first purely abstract painting) wrote a treatise on art, which is what I always found interesting. He felt that when you go see a great work of art—maybe it's Rembrandt or a Renaissance, or whatever—for it to really be successful when you watch it, you are now in direct communication with the artist.

"That artist has created something in his mind that is meaningful to him for a lot of reasons, and maybe a hundred-some-odd years later, when you look at it, you are now in communication with that artist through that work of art if it works for you. He is living through the painting and he is saying something in there, and it may be totally silly, it could be nothing, but he has said something to you. You buy things like that because it moves you; otherwise, there's no point in buying anything."

Weitzenhoffer has been moved more by Kandinsky's work than perhaps any other artist. In 1965, he fell hard for one of Kandinsky's paintings that came up for sale in a public auction at Christie's Auction House in New York City, but he was outbid by a gallery in London. "I knew the dealer because my mother had done some business with him in the past, and I asked him if he would sell, assuming he had purchased it to resell. He said he really couldn't stand it because he didn't like modern pictures."

They struck a deal. Weitzenhoffer got a loan from Liberty Bank in Oklahoma City to buy the Kandinsky for 10 percent more than what the dealer had paid for it. "It was all about the personal communication I had with that painting," he said. "I don't feel that way about many other things, but that particular one I do. If the house catches on fire, the Kandinsky will be the first one to be saved, perhaps before the children. Just kidding."

So there he was at his first crossroads in life, sitting on the sofa at his childhood home near a painting by Monet which was over the fireplace, trying to decide between going to New York to sell masterpieces and maybe see some more of the world, or doing PR for the Oklahoma health department. It wasn't the theatre, but then it wasn't that far from Broadway, either. Something to keep in the back of his mind. Such a no-brainer, really.

He took the job, moved to New York and temporarily got a suite at the Savoy Plaza in Manhattan. He was determined to be successful if he could first learn how to make it in New York, which was not guaranteed. The turbulent 1960s had arrived and New York was becoming center of the universe for both good and bad. They were twisting all night at the Peppermint Lounge when the decade rolled in. Then came the World's Fair, miniskirts, and the launching of Beatlemania as the Beatles first touched foot on American soil on Feb. 7, 1964, in New York City. New York, to its consternation, also got a flood of other immigrants, engendering white flight to the suburbs. The loss of blue-collar jobs in the textile and shipping industries ushered in profound social and political changes. Harlem, the center of African American culture and commerce, was also becoming better known for violence and slums. And right after Weitzenhoffer arrived, the city found itself in the middle of what was called The Blackout of 1965 which struck at the evening rush hour, trapping more than 800,000 riders in the city's subways. All told, it covered 80,000 miles of the Northeast and parts of Canada and left New York in the dark for more than 13 hours.

The five boroughs of New York City had a population of about 7.8 million in 1965, but for the first two years he was there, Weitzenhoffer was exceedingly lonely. He didn't date. Nor did he fit in with the college crowd that got together at the Hamptons on the weekends. "New York was a tough city and I wasn't socially friendly with the families I knew there," he said. "After two years, I got tired of spending my weekends going to all-night movie theatres. The problem was I hadn't found New York yet."

It got so bad he almost went home to Oklahoma. As if he needed extra incentive, Boyd Gunning, the director of the University of Oklahoma Foundation, even told him he would train him to take over his role at the foundation. Max had all but accepted Gunning's offer when his mother told him not to, in the plainest language possible, before closing the conversation with the admonition that he belonged where he was. It was the first time she had said much of anything about his direction in life. He was completely caught off guard, but he took her advice and stayed in New York for another 30 years.

The first few years were spent traveling back and forth to Paris and London meeting with artists and acquiring new works for the Findlays, who specialized in modern art and French Impressionism. One day, while perusing some art galleries on South Molton Street in London, Weitzenhoffer stepped into good fortune when he set foot in Gimpel Fils which was founded in 1946 by Charles and Peter Gimpel. Their father Fils, who was French, owned a large gallery in Paris before World War II. It was eventually seized by the Nazis and Fils and his wife Kay briefly took refuge in the South of France before Fils was killed after joining the French resistance. Peter and Charles made their way to England where Peter joined the British army and became a staff officer for Field Marshal Bernard Montgomery during World War II. Charles, meanwhile, became one of the most famous spies for England, parachuting into France more than a dozen times on clandestine missions. Along the way he was captured once and met his future wife, who also was a spy for the Allies. The Gimpel family war-time narrative was straight out of a war movie and their courage and sacrifice added substance to the post-war Europe Weitzenhoffer had been fascinated by in the summer of '57.

When he first entered the Gimpel Brothers' London gallery, Max was hoping to find something by artist Ben Nicholson and was disappointed to be told none of his work was on display. Instead, Peter Gimpel led him into

Kandinsky had it right

Max, second from left, with Kay, Renee and Peter Gimpel at their New York City gallery.

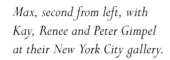

Kandinsky had it right

another room where "Purple Poodle in a Trance" by artist Alan David was for sale. Weitzenhoffer saw something in it and bought it on the spot, paying $4,500, which at the time was not pocket change. "My negotiating style is the one I learned from David Findlay," Weitzenhoffer said. "When he went to a gallery to buy something for resale, he would just say, 'What is our parachute price? And when you give it to me, I'm going to take it or leave it.' That was the end of the negotiation."

Weitzenhoffer left with more than a painting as that chance meeting with Peter Gimpel led to a business partnership. Within a year's time, Max and the Gimpels opened the Gimpel and Weitzenhoffer Art Gallery on Madison Avenue in New York City. The Gimpel brothers furnished the art and Max provided the building with money from the trust fund his grandmother left him. "The Findlay Gallery was getting boring, and I was thinking that the Gimpel family was so interesting that we should have a business together," said Weitzenhoffer.

Max would have never survived as an art dealer—too much small talk and standing around to suit him. But the artists he met in the process did

Fran and Max on Madison Avenue.

give him a newfound appreciation and admiration for sacrifice and hard work, which later translated to the stage. Few, if any, of the artists he met were products of colleges that required degrees to elevate one's work. Instead, they channeled their emotions and their talent to create something that none of us have ever thought about before. "They started at a certain age and they used their own talent and their own hard work to separate themselves from other talented people," Weitzenhoffer said.

Of all the artists he worked with, Max was closest to British sculptor Barbara Hepworth, who was represented by the Gimpels. Weitzenhoffer often visited her at her studio at St. Ives, a picturesque seaside port on the southern tip of the British coastline, and the two corresponded until shortly before her death in 1975. She gave him several of her pieces, and he in turn purchased a number of pieces from her, including "Two Figures," a bronze sculpture that was cast in an edition of seven copies. He paid $19,000 for it in 1971 and donated it to the Fred Jones Jr. Museum of Art on the University of Oklahoma campus that same year. Now valued at about $3 million, it stands just inside the museum entrance, as close to sunlight as possible so that it will serve as a visible sign of the artistic quality the university represents.

Other works donated by Weitzenhoffer include two oil paintings—"Big Solid Sender" by Alan Davie and "Ruins of Rome" by Lowell Nesbitt—as well as "Phenomena Great Divide," an acrylic work by Paul Jenkins.

The principal reason Weitzenhoffer knew he was not cut out to be an art dealer was because he could not look at a piece of art as money in the bank. "I couldn't recognize something as a potentially important piece, so if I didn't personally like it, I might go on a tirade and sell it," he said. That is what happened to the Basquiat he purchased for about $1,000 in the late

Kandinsky had it right

'80s and basically gave away a couple of years later. It has since risen in value to about $15 million.

What he lacked in icy resolve when it came to the art of the art deal, he made up for in other ways. In a letter to Max's mother, Kay Gimpel, the matriarch of her family, wrote that she found Max to be tremendously charming and savored what she called "his brand of humour, of detachment allied with real dedication to his work and profession, his maturity of approach to lots of burning art problems, his vertebrate gentleness—his zest and enjoyment of life."

He had truly come a long way since the 8th grade when his English teacher gave him an achievement grade of 77 and said of him: "Max has the ability to do much higher work than the above grade would indicate. He has imagination and insight and will do well if he will try to apply them on a more adult level than has been seen heretofore. There has been little thoughtful participation in discussion, although he has many talents and interests, and he will, I am sure, soon develop into a mature student of high caliber."

Despite his reluctance to chat up patrons who did not interest him, the gallery did accent some of Max's finest features, which did not go unnoticed by one man. Joseph Hirshhorn was described by the *New York Times* upon his death in 1982 as a man of money and adventure, one of the shrewdest prospectors of gold, uranium and oil of his day as well as the founder and benefactor of the museum in Washington that bears his name."

Hirshhorn admired contemporary art, particularly sculptures, and routinely viewed exhibits at the Gimpel/Weitzenhoffer gallery, where he and Max occasionally interacted. Weitzenhoffer was still single, although he had long since discovered something a lot better to do on the weekends than frequent movie houses by himself. Eventually, Hirshhorn slipped into the conversation that he had someone he wanted Max to meet.

Frances Shapiro was a striking young woman from Louisville, KY, tall and willowy with a hint of a Southern accent that made her self-conscious. In truth, it only magnified the appreciation others had for her. Fluent in French, she had an undergraduate degree from the University of Pennsylvania and a master's degree in Art History from Columbia University. Hirshhorn had employed her to manage his extensive art collection.

There was much to like about Frances, who went on in life to have a distinguished career as an art historian and whose work culminated with the publishing of The *Havemeyers: Impressionism Comes to America*, which was described as a rollicking, behind-the-scenes account of taste in 19th century America, of beautiful paintings bought and sold, and of the collecting activities of the extraordinary couple, Louisine and H.O. Havemeyer. The story began when Louisine Elder, not yet Mrs. H.O. Havemeyer, had the good fortune as a young girl to make friends with Mary Cassatt in Paris

and brought back home the first Degas and the first Monet to reach America. Later, her husband became equally enthralled with the modern French school of Impressionism and put his growing fortune behind their acquisition; thus, the famous Havemeyer Collection was born.

Hirshhorn, the matchmaker, was correct in his assumption that there was something special about her that might appeal to this young art dealer and vice versa, so Hirschhorn sent her to the gallery on some pretense, where the two met.

As setups go, it was not a slam dunk. Frances and Max dated a few times, then broke it off as each of them had somebody else in mind. About a year later they ran into each other on the street, started talking, and within a few weeks were living together in Max's apartment on 64th Street. "She had to break off an engagement and I had to help get rid of the wedding presents," Weitzenhoffer said. "She had her wedding dress made at Bergdorf's. It went into the basement in the original box and was not removed until I sold the apartment in 1995. She always referred to it as the one Miss Havisham would be wearing in *Great Expectations*."

The two had a lot in common—art, politics, the world in general. They spent their summers in France, among other stops, and over time became something of a celebrity couple in Manhattan, bridging the theatrical and

Kandinsky had it right

"Some of our best wines are Italian."

"My wife Fran cooks wiener schnitzel and sauerbraten like a Rhine maiden. But some of our best wines are Italian.

"I've been around paintings and wine for as long as I can remember. When Fran and I are not working, which is admittedly rare, we entertain friends and Fran cooks. A meal is nothing without wine. It's like a frame without a painting.

"We drink many Italian wines. Last week we drank a vintage red and a sparkling white wine that were master-pieces."

For a free vintage chart and guide to the great Italian wines, with an explanation of Italy's strict D.O.C. wine quality laws, send your name and address to Italian Wine Promotion Center 1 World Trade Center New York, N.Y. 10048.

Max and Fran Weitzenhoffer
Gimpel & Weitzenhoffer Art Gallery, N.Y.C.

art worlds. He called her his "other personality" because she had a knack for entertaining and the ability to light up a room in a way he could not. "Mostly, everybody wanted to be around her," he said. "Even though I brought nothing to the table, they had to take me as well."

At the age of 20 she had the composure to interview Picasso at his French studio and the sophistication to walk up to Laurence Olivier when he was sitting alone across the aisle from Max and her at a play and completely charm him. She was intelligent and gracious, but opinionated and funny.

For many years she was the protégée and professional associate of John Rewald, the pioneer authority of French Impressionism and edited three of his books: *Aspects of Monet, Studies in Impressionism* and *Studies in Post-Impressionism.*

New York publisher Paul Gottlieb, the noted editor in chief of Harry N. Abrams, the dominant art book publishing house in the country at the time, met Fran over lunch in 1981 with Rewald, Fritz Landshoff (one of Gottlieb's senior colleagues), and Fritz's wife Rini. A lively discussion ensued, and the foursome repaired to the Weitzenhoffer's apartment, where Fran, a physical fitness advocate, cheerily demonstrated several new exercises for the group to consider.

"John and Rini began to follow her exercises, but Fritz refused to participate in this needless waste of energy," Gottlieb later related. "He was 80 years old by then and still working full time. Instead, he sat down, spied a thick black binder containing a manuscript and began to read. It was Fran's remarkable doctoral dissertation about the amazing Havemeyers who brought Impressionism to America."

Gottlieb said he was ashamed to say that it took him six months to get around to finish reading it but when he did he was quick to offer her a contract for her first book. "That moment marked the beginning of a wonderful publishing experience and the beginning of a friendship," he said.

It was hard work for Fran to turn a scholar's thesis into a book that could appeal to a wider and less knowledgeable audience, but upon its publication, Fran was established as an authority in the art world. Avis Berman in an ecstatic review in "Art News" suggested that Frank's book serve as the basis of the Metropolitan Museum of Art to arrange an exhibition of some of the greatest treasures of the Havemeyer bequest, which took five years to come to fruition.

"Unfortunately, the letter to Fran written by the museum's director came too late for her to read it. By that time, Fran was in the grip of her final illness," Gottlieb wrote.

"Fran knew how to have good times—parties at home, a wicked bit of gossip, shopping for her striking and unusual get-ups, tea at the Savoy before we all attended with Max the London opening of *Aspects of Love*. Fran was enormously proud of Max's accomplishments.

Kandinsky had it right

Clara Weitzenhoffer and CBS anchorman Dan Rather.

"In the summer of 1986, after Fran and her friend Bannie McHenry arrived after a hysterical train ride from the south of France to visit me in the Loire Valley, we did the great chateaux and drank a lot of wine as well. Later Fran and I drove south, stopping to see the town of Nevers, which Fran had heard of but had never seen and where her mother taught school many years before. We drove on to the cathedral of Autun where Fran marveled as early morning sun, shining through stained glass windows, threw miniature rainbows against the ancient stone walls.

"It was on that trip I learned of Fran's earlier illness. It seemed so long ago—it never occurred to me that it might return so cruelly.

Thanks to some aggressive treatment, it was thought that Fran had beaten breast cancer when she was first diagnosed with the disease in 1977. But it returned with vengeance in 1990. She died in 1991 at the age of 46. Dan Rather, who was at the height of his broadcasting career at the time as the CBS anchorman, and his wife were good friends of Fran and Max, and it was Rather who delivered her eulogy at her memorial service.

"My friends, I am going to do that which I know Fran would do for me," he said in his opening. "Our beloved and loving Fran, daughter, wife, and friend, died where womanhood's morning almost touches noon and while the shadows were still falling towards the west. She was still rising up when the down draft caught her. She died while yet in love with life and raptured with the world. She passed to silence and dust, she fell into that dreamless sleep that kisses down the eyelids still, while she was still in her prime. And, what a prime! Tall, tenacious and talented, the girl from Kentucky who became the woman from New York.

"This brave and tender woman in every storm of life was oak and rock, but in the sunshine, she was vine and flower. She was the friend of all heroic

Kandinsky had it right

104

and tender souls. She loved the beautiful and color, form, and music often touched her to tears. Fran sided with the weak and with willing hand gave always, more than her share. With loyal heart and with the purest hand, she faithfully discharged all trusts of relatives and friends. She specialized in listening love. She was a worshiper of freedom and a friend of the oppressed, not in the political or ideological ways—in artistic and human ways. I believe that Fran believed happiness was the only good, reason the only torch, humanity the only religion, and love its leader."

The one person Fran could not charm was Max's mother. And Max was not up to the task of winning over Fran's father Dr. David Shapiro, either, so they were a perfect couple in that sense. Fran's mother had died of breast cancer by the time Max came along, and Fran hardly ever saw her father after that, while Max never saw him. "He didn't like me at all, which was just perfect because when Thanksgiving came, I never had to be around any in-laws I didn't want to spend the day with."

Max's mother, meanwhile, did not treat Fran any better. She never spoke to her daughter-in-law until Fran was diagnosed with breast cancer in 1977 and only managed a few words after that point. Fran called her mother-in-law 'her royal shortness' while Max said his mother only started talking to Fran after she thought she might expire soon."

"My mother had an unpleasant side to her historically," Max allowed. "She thought Fran's family, who was Jewish, was from the wrong side of the Oder River (which formed the border between Germany and Eastern Europe and which was looked down upon by some German Jews)."

Max and Fran's impromptu wedding in 1976 personified how they lived life. They had attended a University of Oklahoma football game in Norman on Thanksgiving Day. From there, Max was to join his mother in La Jolla for the holidays, while Fran was on her way to see her family in Florida. It is not clear what precipitated it, but they decided to get married in Dallas, Texas, which did not require a waiting period. In an ode to his warped sense of humor, Weitzenhoffer assumes Oklahoma must have won the game, putting him in a good enough mood to get married. After the ceremony, the two immediately went their separate ways and didn't bother to tell anyone they were officially married until months later. "I think my mother didn't speak to me for years because she was mad that I didn't immediately tell her."

Often, there seemed to be little room inside him for sentimentality. Maybe that's because his mind was crowded with something else, something he could never get out of his head.

Kandinsky had it right

Bernie Jacobs. I was fortunate to learn from the best. I was privileged to have been mentored by someone who was recognized at being the best at what they did and then to become friends with him. I got to learn things from him that he didn't tell anyone else and to understand the business from the master. I drew strength from simply being in his presence.

Bernie Jacobs, 1981. Photo by Adele Hodge, courtesy The Shubert Archive.

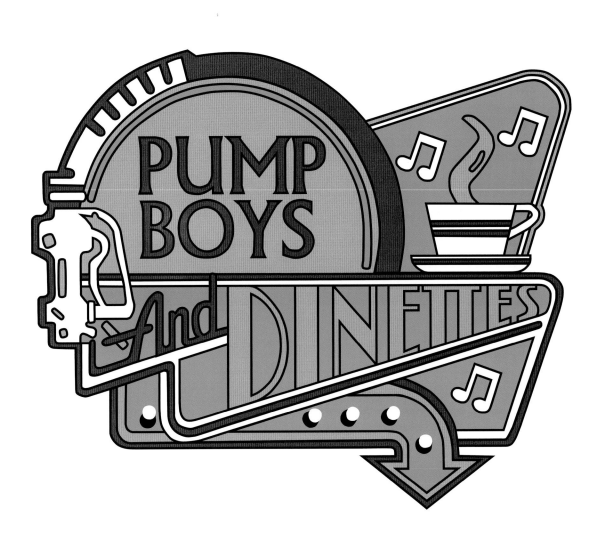

**N**ot long ago Max Weitzenhoffer was walking Marlowe, his latest Dalmatian in a long line of the breed, when he stopped and looked down at the road to reflect on the one he took to get there. The public record will show that he ran through a few red lights along the way and navigated some winding curves, regularly exceeding the speed limit in the fastest car he could afford to buy and driving with the fearlessness of a Grand Prix driver on top of that. But the more he thought about his life, the more he realized there was only one word for it—luck.

"By masterstroke, I couldn't get into any university I applied to coming out of high school, because if I had, the road would have been different," he explained. "But the truth is I would have gone to any of those other places in a minute, so sometimes it is a series of luck. I always think luck is more important than anything else. The other part, knowing what I do—my secret is when I don't know something, I hire somebody that does know it."

Luck might have entered into the game when the Gimpel/Weitzenhoffer Gallery was under investigation by the Internal Revenue Service in 1977, suspected of writing off an excessive amount of losses. The IRS considered the gallery to be more of a hobby for Weitzenhoffer than it was an actual business, which would have drastically increased his tax liability. "There was an Internal Revenue guy in my basement for a month (auditing the books) and I wasn't happy, so I hired a new lawyer and an accountant, Kenneth Starr." Starr's intervention saved the day for Weitzenhoffer and he went on to play a crucial role in Max's success as a producer. Was that strictly luck?

It would not be proper to call it lucky, but it was fortuitous for both Nimax Theatres and Weitzenhoffer when Michael Jackson died after Nimax began presenting the play *Thriller Live,* a celebration of the legendary pop star's musical talents. That was on June 25, 2009, and eight years later *Thriller Live* is still filling the seats at Nimax's Apollo Theatre. That was all luck.

Lucky is the word he also uses to describe the events leading up to his marriage to the two women in his life. His good fortune seems to amaze him to this day. "That's where I was really lucky," he emphasized. "How I found two unique women who have been so instrumental in my life in such a positive way is truly a mystery to me." It could be claimed that Weitzenhoffer might have been considered a catch in his own right when it came to marriage, somewhat medicating his assertion that all the luck was on his side of the ledger. No matter how it came to pass, his two marriages shaped both his career and his destiny in ways that cannot be underestimated.

In the end, perhaps nothing demonstrated pure luck like the phone call from his mother in the fall of 1970, telling Max he should investigate a cute little mystery she had just seen in London, *Sleuth*. If that wasn't all about luck, at the very least it was a classic case of luck meeting opportunity.

Weitzenhoffer never really knew why his mother made the suggestion, as she didn't seem enamored with the fact that he had designs on the theatre. Yet when she traveled, a night at the theatre was almost always on her agenda and it seemed she always had something to say about the show. Maybe that's all there was to it. It's also possible that she knew her son well enough to know that selling pictures would not hold his interest for very long.

Timely information about plays on the other side of the Atlantic was then a lot harder to come by than it is now but Weitzenhoffer, for some reason, became as consumed with *Sleuth* as its audience was in trying to figure out how the suspense thriller would end. Written by Anthony Shaffer, the play is set in England in the Wiltshire manor house of Andrew Wyke, an acclaimed mystery writer whose character was inspired by famous composer Stephen Sondheim. Wyke's home reflects his obsession with inventions and his deceptions of fiction along with his fascination with games and game-playing. Wyke lures his wife's lover, Miles Tindle, to the house and convinces him to stage a robbery of her jewelry, which leaves the audience totally unsure of who is staring back at them when they peer into the looking glass as Wyke and Tindle try to out 'who-dunnit' each other.

His mother's little nudge had worked and by the next day Max's curiosity had already turned caution into a crusade. He started thumbing through the theatrical index and came up with the names of *Sleuth's* producers: Helen Bonfils, Morton Gottlieb and Michael White, although Gottlieb was the one in charge. Weitzenhoffer had never met him, but it didn't prevent him from immediately placing a call. Max had obviously not yet seen the play, but none of that seemed to matter. He just had a good feeling about it. "I'd like to put up $6,000," (which would equate to about $40,000 in 2018) Max said to Mr. Gottlieb. As quickly as he blurted out a number, Gottlieb made it clear that they didn't need any more investors. Undeterred, Weitzenhoffer kept talking and somehow earned an invitation from Morty to join him for lunch at the Yale Club, a private club in midtown Manhattan.

At some point during lunch, Gottlieb caved in and Weitzenhoffer suddenly found himself in show business. Directed by Clifford Williams, *Sleuth* opened at the Music Box Theatre on Broadway on Nov. 12, 1970, with Anthony Quayle starring as Andrew Wyke and Keith Baxter as Milo Tindle. Baxter received the Drama Desk Award for Outstanding Performance, and Williams and lighting designer William Ritman also received Tony nominations. *Sleuth* rang up 1,222 performances on Broadway and was made into a movie in 1972. It seemed that Max had talked himself into something big his first time out of the gate: His investment generated him

Morty Gottleib

a $60,000 return, equating to about $400,000 in today's dollars. It was the kind of nest egg that could not be overstated because disappointment could always find you on Broadway, where the goal was more about avoiding flops than it was to get rich. "What I learned is that if you are not aware of your own limitations, you can't make it," Weitzenhoffer said.

Morty Gottlieb was the perfect teacher for Max in that regard. So, too, was actor and friend Alfred Drake, who took a liking to Weitzenhoffer and opened doors for him on Broadway. Then came his accountant and business advisor Kenneth Starr, who helped him cultivate an image and attract investors. Finally, there was Bernard Jacobs, who taught Weitzenhoffer more do's and don'ts than he could ever have learned on his own. All played key roles in his success; all were strong, straight-forward men, which seems to be another prerequisite if one hopes to have any longevity on Broadway.

When he died in 2009 at the age of 88, Gottlieb was described in the *New York Times* as an old-fashioned producer because he devoted his career largely to championing original scripts, shepherding them step-by-step from the page to the stage and, when possible, on to the screen. He was not a promoter of high art. But he had good instincts for what Broadway audiences, if not always Broadway critics, would admire.

He was revered by investors for paying them back in timely fashion, something Weitzenhoffer had already learned in the art world. According to the *Times*, Gottlieb produced Bernard Slade's *Tribute*, starring Jack Lemmon. The previews were so successful that Morty wrote checks to his investors at the opening-night party. And Gottlieb's concern for other people's money extended well beyond normal bounds. "When I worked for him, you had to reuse the envelope," his niece told the *Times*. Gottlieb never had a car

Better lucky than good

and got to most places he wanted to go on a bicycle. And Weitzenhoffer remembers that if he invited him somewhere for lunch, Morty would never stop eating. His office was bare-bones and his house in the country was furnished with set pieces from the shows he had produced. "But everybody liked Morty," Max emphasized.

As reported by the *Times*, two of Gottlieb's earlier plays—*The Killing of Sister George*, a semi-farcical drama by Frank Marcus about an outrageously self-centered and wrathful radio star, which moved from London to Broadway in 1966, and *Lovers,* a two-part 1969 comedy by Brian Friel that starred Art Carney—were nominated for best play Tony Awards. Other notable credits from early in his career included *Enter Laughing*, Joseph Stein's comedy based on a pseudo-memoir novel by Carl Reiner. *Enter Laughing* played 419 performances in 1963 and 1964 and propelled Alan Arkin to fame as well as Joseph Heller's satire *We Bombed in New Haven* in 1968.

Morton Edgar Gottlieb was born in Brooklyn on May 2, 1921, and graduated from Erasmus Hall High School. After studying drama at Yale he entered the theatre business as a press agent, later working on several shows as company manager or general manager. His first venture as a producer was a 1953 summer stock production of *Arms and the Man*, which happened to be the last stage appearance by Marlon Brando.

Gottlieb, a talkative, sociable man who won a Bachelor of the Year award given out by a popular line of men's toiletries in 1968, never married. Because he seemed to prefer "middlebrow" material, Gottlieb was considered to be more popular with his audiences than he was the critics. "The Broadway theatre is the only place in the world where the easiest way to break in is by starting at the top," he once said. "You don't need experience, you don't need a license, you don't need money. All you need is chutzpah. You call all the agents and say, 'Here I am—a producer!'"

That line could easily have been written for Weitzenhoffer because Gottlieb gave him an introduction to how shows were produced on Broadway that he would not otherwise have had. "He let me meet the people who worked for him on the show and he let me work in his office all the time," Max said. "After he did *Sleuth,* he gave me another script to read."

The script was called *Same Time, Next Year*. New Jersey accountant George Peters and Doris, a housewife from Oakland, California, met at an inn on the Mendocino County coast in Northern California in 1951, where they had an affair after which they agreed to meet once a year despite the fact both were married to others and had six children between them. It grew into much more than a tryst as, over time, they shared everything about their lives, the good and the bad, and supported one another like spouses would.

Weitzenhoffer decided against getting involved in what they thought would turn out to be a quirky love story. "I read it, and I think I told Morty that it was just a TV show. The play *Same Time, Next Year* was a smash hit, both on Broadway and on film. When it opened at the Brooks Atkinson Theatre with Ellen Burstyn and Charles Grodin, *New York Times* critic Clive Barnes wrote, "Do not put off till tomorrow what you can do today. Get tickets for *Same Time, Next Year* . . . It is the funniest comedy about love and adultery to come Broadway's way in years."

Weitzenhoffer refused to take the critic's advice. "I never went to see it, because I was so annoyed that I had turned it down," he confessed.

But mistakes are something you learn to live with in the theatre. The standing joke among Broadway producers was that if you had a big hit, the only thing people wanted to know was, "What are you going to do next?" While Weitzenhoffer did have an almost unheard-of return on his investment in *Sleuth*, what mattered more was the unlimited access Gottlieb gave him into his thought process. "I worked in his office all the time," Max said. "He didn't have any partners, anyway, so I got to meet a lot of people. That's how I got started."

It was Gottlieb who taught Max how to deal with investors; unfortunately, no show would ever take its first breath without investors. For one thing, he never asked anybody for more than $6,000 because in those days, investors could take 50 percent of their losses as a tax deduction if the show failed. Besides, $6,000 wasn't a big deal to most of them. "And he never asked for money from people who would have to stress about it," Max added. "He wanted it to be something they were interested in and liked to do. So he might have 30 investors, and because his shows almost always made money, he had a lot of people wanting to invest with him—people like me."

Foremost, Morty was not a cheat, Max said. "But that was a whole different generation of producers and Broadway was a different place," he continued. After a couple of big shows that had been improperly financed by others went under, the Security and Exchange Commission became suspicious about how shows were being capitalized in general, which led to tighter rules governing the investment of Broadway productions. "Eventually, Morty just stopped doing them because shows got so expensive and his style of producing was on the way out," Max said.

What he also learned from hanging around Gottlieb was that it was almost as important to get rid of the wrong people as it was to find the right people in the first place. "Every time you get ready to do a show, you have a large number of creative people who move out of the area in which they are creating," Weitzenhoffer said. "I mean, if you are dealing with lighting/designers/choreographers, invariably they will always try to inflict on you things that will either not work or is really none of their business in the sense that they will have suggestions about the show, suggestions about what the other people are doing instead of paying attention to what they should be doing in their element.

Better lucky than good

113

"I think that's one of the real problems with the theatre in that a lot of shows that shouldn't fail do so because the influences of people you hired are incorrect and you are not able to turn the production around."

Weitzenhoffer's best example of why it is important to get it right the first time is the one show where he and co-producer Frank Milton got it oh, so wrong. *Harold and Maude*, which was a hit in Paris and on the big screen, closed on Broadway after a measly four performances.

Coming on the heels of Weitzenhoffer's triumph with *Dracula*, *Harold and Maude* was more than a heaping spoonful of reality. It was more like swallowing the Mississippi River in one gulp. "I think when you are just getting started and you end up with some gigantic hit and a Tony Award, you suddenly decide in your mind that you now know what you are doing," Max said. "And, then, when you proceed to reverse yourself and do the worst straight play flop in the history of Broadway, you realize you don't know what the f--- you are doing."

Weitzenhoffer and Milton had seen *Harold and Maude* performed at the Dorsey in Paris with Madeleine Renaud. Director Jean-Louis Barrault had directed it and one of the decisions he made was to use a bare stage. When they got back to New York, Weitzenhoffer and Milton's first mistake was to determine that the play wouldn't work on Broadway without scenery, which meant their concept was wrong from the beginning.

"Then we decided we needed a star, so we went to see Katharine Hepburn and she didn't like the idea that the play had this relationship between this young boy and the older woman, an implied relationship," Max explained. "She wanted that element changed, which is a key element; it's what the show is about. We had a talk with Colin Higgins (the playwright) and decided we couldn't change it as it wouldn't be the same show any longer. So that eliminated her."

Finally, they hired well-respected British actress Glynis Johns and added Robert Lewis, who was famous as the director of *Brigadoon*. "We thought since *Brigadoon* was a fantasy that this would be a good project for Lewis because *Harold and Maude* was also a fantasy. Anyway, we got into rehearsal and Glynis called me at 2–3 a.m. and said, 'I can't work with him (Lewis).'"

She said that her interpretation of the part and the way she wanted to play it were not reconcilable with the way Lewis was interpreting it. "I was in bed at home and I think Glynis had had a couple of drinks to get up the courage to call me. I said, 'Glynis, it's late at night, we're tired, I know what you're saying, and I need to call Frank and we'll discuss it and I'll talk to you tomorrow.' So, then I called Frank and he says, 'Well, we've got this director and it's important because he has this concept, so we have to let her go.' And I thought, 'Okay'. Of course, I should have let the director go, but I didn't want to hurt him because I was too much of a novice then."

In search of another star, Max and Frank flew to Palm Springs, California,

Katharine Hepburn

Better lucky than good

to consult with Mary Martin, who suggested the best person to play the role was her closest friend, Janet Gaynor, who won an Academy Award but who had never been on the stage before.

"The show's failure had nothing to do with her performance, but it had to do with the direction, among other things," Max asserted. "We just hired all the wrong people. The cast was good, but we couldn't overcome the direction of the process."

It was Weitzenhoffer's fifth show—his first and fourth, *Sleuth* and *Dracula*, respectively, had been big hits; his second and third, *Tickles by Tucholsky*, which played off-Broadway, and *Going Up*, were not embraced by audiences, although they had their artistic moments. *Harold and Maude*, however, taught him more than he learned from all the others combined. "I think what it taught me is that you don't learn anything from a hit," he said. "A hit covers up all the mistakes, and the thing you also learn is that every time you do a show something will come up that you've never seen before and that is a potential disaster."

For example, there was the time when he and fellow producer and friend Jim Freydberg were preparing a show off Broadway and hired a reportedly top-notch scene designer, who, as it turned out, did not know how to design much of anything. "We were in a new theatre off Broadway and when we were ready to move the set on stage, it was too big. Then, when the scene designer was screwing around trying to adjust the set, he knocked over something, which tripped the sprinkler system, which then flooded the theatre."

The other takeaway for Weitzenhoffer from *Harold and Maude* was that if a show fails, there should be no scapegoating: "The producer is ultimately responsible for all the people who screwed up. I mean, yes, they didn't do their job the way they were supposed to, but it's the producer's fault because I should have known better in the beginning."

In a way, Weitzenhoffer had simply forgotten his producer's lines when he fired the wrong person in *Harold and Maude* because award-winning actor, singer and director Alfred Drake had laid out some ground rules for Max to follow when they first met in 1974. They were introduced by a mutual friend who told Max that Drake might give him some guidance about a new show that had caught Weitzenhoffer's eye. "The University of Oklahoma had done an original musical based on the *Wizard of Id*. It had gotten really good reviews, and I thought the music was terrific," Max said. "They had sent me a tape and everything. I didn't know anything about producing. At the same time, I had all this music on tape for a show. I barely knew Alfred Drake, so a mutual friend got Alfred to come up to my apartment and listen to the tape. I said, 'I got this great new musical, and I really would like your opinion, so I played him a selection of songs.'"

Drake took it all in, then came back with one question:

Alfred Drake and Max on opening night at the theatre.

"Do you know why you like this music?"

"Yeah, because it's really good," Weitzenhoffer replied, "And, it's by a young composer and lyricist with a lot of talent."

"That may be true," Drake said. "But the problem with the scoring is that all the music sounds like the music that comes from hit musicals of other shows, which is a normal mistake that all young lyricists and composers make. That's because once they start writing, the first things that come into their mind are things they've heard in the past. So, the numbers they start compiling are numbers from their memory bank."

Drake told Max to play one of their numbers.

"I played it and then he would start singing along with something that sounded exactly like that number, but it was from a show a long time ago," Max said. "It had nothing to do with plagiarizing or anything; they weren't really aware they were doing it because they thought what they were pulling out of their head was totally original."

Thankfully, Weitzenhoffer was spared from investing in what would have been a dud. Better yet, Drake's blunt assessment of Max's inability to spot a major flaw in a number didn't faze him. Instead, it became the foundation on which a lasting friendship was built.

Drake was born as Alfred Capurro on Oct. 7, 1914, in New York City, the son of parents who emigrated from Recco, Italy. He began his Broadway career while still a student at Brooklyn College and is best known for his leading roles in original Broadway productions of *Oklahoma!*; *Kiss Me, Kate*; and *Kismet*; and for playing Marshall Blackstone in the original production of *Babes in Arms*, in which he sang the title song. He won Tony awards for his roles in *Kismet* and *Kean* and in 1990 received a Tony Award for Excellence in the Theatre.

When Robert Viagas wrote his book *I'm the Greatest Star*—subtitled *Broadway's Top Musical Legends from 1900 to Today*—he selected 20 men to profile and made Drake one of his choices. "Why not? Drake routinely drew raves from critics, but the sweetest notice might well have come from Richard Watts in the *New York Post*," Viagas said. "On that December night in 1953 after he'd seen Drake's new musical he decided, "He's at his best in *Kismet*, which is saying a lot." Writer Peter Filichia wrote this of Drake: "Musical theatre authorities always cite what a landmark song "Oh, What a Beautiful Mornin'" was—but let's not forget who strolled out on that almost bare St. James stage to sing it. The show's authors, no less than Rodgers and Hammerstein, when writing *The King and I* eight years later, wanted Drake to play their monarch. He turned it down because it didn't contain enough songs to suit him. Drake did later play the part when Yul Brynner went on vacation, but that was a poor consolation prize given the popularity of *The King and I*. "He told me that he had made a terrible mistake by not taking the part," Weitzenhoffer said.

Chita Rivera, Drake's co-star in *Zenda*, a 1963 Vernon Duke-Martin Charnin musical that opened and closed in California, revealed a little-known fact about him, Filichia wrote. "As I went to the first day of rehearsals," she says, "I was so excited at the thought of meeting the great Alfred Drake, whom I'd seen to be so sexy and dashing in so many shows. And when I came into the room, I was astonished to see that Alfred was actually a very short man. He never seemed it on stage, and that," she says with a decisive finger-point, "is what you call stage presence."

Drake had that and much more. And by the time Weitzenhoffer came along late in his life, Drake was prepared to share a lot of what he knew with Max. He showed Max around the town and was even able to get him into the Players' Club, a private social club. Founded in 1888, Edwin Booth, the greatest American actor of his time, purchased a Gothic Revival-style mansion facing Gramercy Park and commissioned architect Stanford White to transform it into a certain club "for the promotion of social intercourse between the representative members of the dramatic profession and the kindred professions of literature, painting, sculpture and music, and the patrons of the arts."

Sitting at a table next to James Cagney seemed a lot more in line with what Max wanted out of life than waiting for the paint to dry at the art gallery. Just as Gottlieb knew what to put on stage to grab an audience, Drake taught Max what *not* to put on stage. "He taught me that when you do a musical, you never put stairs on the set because as soon as you have a stairway, the director immediately wants to stick the star on it, and then they're back somewhere standing or something and the audience is drawn to them, whether they are doing something or not. That's just something some directors don't get anymore."

Max and Fran socialized a lot with Drake as well, to the point that they were like family. And Weitzenhoffer was always a little bit in awe of Drake's stage presence, no matter where he went. "One time we were all going to dinner in the Village before a show and when it came time to pay the bill, the manager told us they didn't take credit cards. Alfred looked at him and said, 'You should have told me that on the telephone when I made the reservation. So, would you like all of us to stay and wash dishes or should I come back tomorrow and pay?'"

Like Weitzenhoffer's foray into art, Kenneth Starr's day job as a money manager was not nearly as appealing to him as the theatre. The year was 1977 and the two were on the threshold of something big. Weitzenhoffer was about to score a Broadway Tony Award as the producer of *Dracula* at the age of 36 when Starr told him he had some extra space where he worked if Max ever wanted to get away from the gallery and concentrate more on the theatre.

It wasn't long before Starr had an even better idea. "How'd you like to

James Cagney

Better lucky than good

118

become president of the Shubert Organization?" he asked Max. That seemed far-fetched to Weitzenhoffer, but he told Starr he might like the idea given that the Shubert Organization was America's oldest professional theatre company. Formed at the end of the 19th century by brothers Sam, Lee and Jacob J. Shubert, the company, which is still in operation, has owned hundreds of theatres, produced more than 500 plays and musicals, and has owned and operated more than 1,000 playhouses across the United States. Since the 1980s, the company's ticketing service has grown to become the leading ticket provider in New York City's thriving theatre industry. By 1916, the Shuberts had become the nation's most important and powerful theatre owners and managers.

Although the company was minimally involved in theatrical production in the 1950s and 1960s, Shubert returned to producing full time in the '70s and had many outstanding and award-winning shows to its credit, including *The Act* (1977) and *Ain't Misbehavin'* (1978). Not surprisingly, much of its success occurred under the leadership of Bernard Jacobs and Gerald Schoenfeld, who were named president and chairman, respectively, in 1973.

"Well, let's see what we can do," Starr offered.

Starr wasn't just reaching for the stars when he made that statement about how far Max could go in the business. The way to get there, Starr decided, was for people to think Max was indeed the wealthy oil tycoon New Yorkers fancied him to be. In many ways, he fit the bill because it was true that his grandfather and father and their wives lived fascinating lives thanks in large part to the oil field. His grandparents and parents were even reasonable facsimiles of the Benedicts in the classic film *Giant*, minus all the land, cattle and Texas braggadocio. *Giant,* made in 1956 and directed by George Stevens, starred Elizabeth Taylor, Rock Hudson and James Dean, who was killed in a car wreck before the film was released. In 2005, it was selected for preservation in the United States National Film Registry by the Library of Congress as being "culturally, historically and aesthetically significant. *Giant* was the epitome of money and power delivered in typical bigger-than-life Texas fashion, sparing the usual civility that distinguishes old money from new money."

Other than his mother's paintings that were hanging without fanfare in four rooms in the Weitzenhoffer home and a couple of Cadillacs in the garage, Max's upbringing was not entirely Benedictesque. In fact, his father often remarked that Oklahoma was a good place to be Jewish because there were too few of their faith to raise any objections at Christmas. Extravagant the Weitzenhoffers weren't.

Yet Starr created a persona for Max that suggested to potential Broadway investors he could afford to spend whatever it took to make a splash. If you discounted the money he would eventually inherit, Max was closer at the time to financially representing what rich Texans call the faux rich—"Big Hat, No Cattle." It didn't hurt, though, that he was well-versed in art and knew his way around Europe as well as any sophisticated New Yorker. "It's the perception of being able to do something that you're not sure you can do," Max said. "That's what life is like in the theatre. It's play acting in a way."

Starr formed several investment companies that focused on theatrical productions, the first blind pool investment companies of their kind in the theatre, Weitzenhoffer said. In the past, investors had largely determined the shows in which they participated, but under the pool plan, Weitzenhoffer selected the shows and took the credit, or blame, depending on the outcome. "Clients went into it recognizing they could lose all their money, because after all, it was an investment pool," Max said. Al Pacino and Mike Nichols were among those who bet on Max's ability to pick a winner, much like his father and grandfather picked a spot in the ground in which to drill for oil.

It turned out well in the end for Weitzenhoffer, who severed ties with Starr in the '80s when "the climate in his office started feeling different," and Starr's interest shifted to investing in Hollywood. That was long before Starr's was accused of operating a $35-million dollar Ponzi scheme with funds entrusted to him by a number of celebrity clients. Starr was indicted on 23 criminal counts, including fraud and money laundering charges, and in 2010 pleaded guilty in federal court. He was sentenced to a seven-and-a-half year prison term in federal prison.

"It's too bad what happened to him," Weitzenhoffer said. "They (the prosecutors) looked at everything we did together and there was nothing there. Ken was probably as brilliant as anybody I've ever been around. In those days, he just wore one old suit, drove an old car and was always reading a book. Ken's problem was one a lot of accountants have—they deal with huge clients who may not treat them well and that begins to hurt after a while, although that's no excuse for breaking the law."

When the chief financial officer of Really Useful Theatres was looking for a major investor, it was Starr who helped Max raise $500,000 overnight to keep the *Phantom* afloat. "That's the best deal I ever made on the stage in theatre."

But it was Bernie Jacobs who paved the way for the best investment Weitzenhoffer ever made—the purchase of the block of London theatres now owned by Nimax.

It wasn't until Weitzenhoffer ran into Jacobs at Sydmonton in 1986 that he began to get to know the man behind the legend. At that point Jacobs had been president of the Shubert Organization for more than 15 years, making him one of the most powerful men in American theatre. Everything that transpired on Broadway for two decades was heavily influenced by his taste.

After that first weekend at Sydmonton with their wives, Max frequently saw Jacobs in London, where Jacobs often met with Lloyd Webber regarding new shows and where Weitzenhoffer spent as much time as he could justify. "Mainly, what I got out of it is you only make money by owning theatres," Weitzenhoffer stated. "That's what he taught me in his mentoring. But I think the rest of the mentoring was in how he operated and the type of relationships he had with his employees. And the other important thing I learned from him is that you always want to align yourself with the most creative people in the business, because they're the ones that will eventually supply you with the product you need for your theatres."

When Max made the rounds with Jacobs, what impressed him most and what has stayed with him longer than anything was the personal relationship he had with his employees, from his box office managers to the ushers. He knew their first names, was familiar with their families and always made them feel like they were part of his family.

Jacobs could also clearly be more bristly than a Brillo pad. Consequently, the darts and digs dropped from the sky without warning. "One day he was talking about Roger Berlin, a very aristocratic and classy man and out of nowhere he asked me if I was Jewish," Max said. "I said, 'Yes, why do you ask?' He said, 'Well, it's just that Roger Berlin always pretends he's not, and I can't figure it out.'"

Jacobs got some laughs out of Jerry Schoenfeld, his Shubert Theatre colleague, too. "To give you an idea of the relationship, one was the president and one was the chairman of the Shubert Organization; Bernie ran the creative side and Jerry ran the real estate end . . . One day Bernie and I were getting ready to go to lunch and I was sitting in Bernie's office and Jerry comes in and says something and then leaves. Bernie's private comment to me was, 'Jerry's head is getting so big he can't get through my door.'"

It was a time on Broadway when competitors could still be partners and that's what happened with Weitzenhoffer, Jacobs and Jimmy Nederlander, who ran the Nederlander Organization, one of the largest theatre owners and producers in the country. "We had had a situation where the three of us went together on *Sunset Boulevard,* Lloyd Webber's touring show," Max said. "The show was opening at the big Shubert house in Los Angeles when Andrew, at the last minute, decided he didn't feel Faye Dunaway was suitable for the part and decided to postpone the whole thing. Now, we're sitting there with a big advance and no star, no nothing. So, we didn't know what to do with all this money that everybody had invested, and we wanted compensation from the next company of *Sunset*, which was a Canadian Company. So, we told them that you just can't decide you're not going to do this and screw us out of the $8 million we had invested."

At a meeting of the three at the Berkeley Hotel in London, Jimmy and Bernie decided that since Max got along better with the *Sunset* than they did, that he would have to be the one to get their money back.

"This is how it went," Weitzenhoffer said. "I called up the head of Really

Useful, and told him I had to talk to him. "When he got there, I said, 'Now, you know the three of us have all this money in the show and you've just closed it. What are we supposed to do?' He said, 'Well, that's your tough luck. That's show business.' I said, 'Well then you have a problem. You have a very distinct problem. I'm just going to tell you in advance.'

"Then I hinted that Jimmy had laid off a large portion of his share of the investment to somebody that may not have been properly registered with the Security and Exchange Commission and that was going to cause a big problem for him, which was a total lie on my part. I then said, 'You can either compensate us in the next production or you'll wind up being sued and have to return all our money, so you need to make up your mind exactly which way you're going.' And then I left."

Really Useful came back with a counter offer. Weitzenhoffer, Jacobs and Nederlander would be able to redeem their investment in another production of *Sunset*. "It ended well, and it had nothing to do with Andrew; it had to do with the company, and it turned out to be a funny story," Max said.

For years, Jacobs had dealt with a heart condition. Finally, one day he called Weitzenhoffer and said he wanted to let Max know he was going to have major surgery the next day.

"I'm very concerned," he said.

"Well, why? Is it necessary?" Max wanted to know.

"Yes," Jacobs said. "The doctor told me I wouldn't live six months if I don't have this heart surgery."

Max responded with a quip, which is the way their game was played. "Well, you've got to have it because you can't leave us with Jerry."

The next day Jacobs was operated on, and the early reports were that it was successful. But then he had a stroke and died.

The obituary in *The New York Times* read, in part:

Acting as producers as well as theatre owners, Mr. Jacobs and his partner have had more to say than anyone else about what shows opened on Broadway—from A Chorus Line to Cats to The Life and Adventures of Nicholas Nickleby to the Pulitzer Prize-winning Glengarry Glen Ross and The Heidi Chronicles. At the same time, they also determined what shows closed in their theatres, and when. Although there are other competitive theatre owners, none approaches the extensive range of theatres and the sweeping authority of the Shuberts. Despite his immense influence, Mr. Jacobs resolutely avoided the spotlight. Bernie was the most unpretentious man I ever met—and this in a field in which names mean everything,' said Dasha Epstein, a Broadway producer and a close friend of Mr. Jacobs and his wife, Betty. 'He was a man who didn't need scenery.' In private, he was known for his sharpness. The producer Albert

Poland said he recalled hearing him on the telephone with Baron de Rothschild, saying angrily, 'I can't give you tickets. I'm in the business of selling tickets.' Then he hung up and explained that the Baron wanted him to donate all the tickets to a performance of Cats for a benefit. 'What is he?' said Mr. Jacobs. 'Just a man with a de in front of his name.'

Even the infallible Bernard Jacobs was not totally flawless, at least when it came to the question of scenery and how little or how much one needed to make a statement. In 1977, when Weitzenhoffer and his partner John Wulp were in search of a theatre to house *Dracula* and made their pitch to Jacobs, his only response was, "Nobody cares about scenery."

In this case, *Dracula* had the last bite.

Better lucky than good

"**A** complete delight. An extravaganza of horror; funny, charming and with a happy touch of serious authenticity. It has style, wit, chic. Frank Langella's 'Dracula' is exquisitely conceived and dashingly executed. Vastly entertaining, it gives Broadway a shot in the arm. A veritable blood transfusion!"
—Clive Barnes

"**E**legant, taut and visually stunning with a powerful, bone-shaking ending. Frank Langella is a stunning figure as Dracula: tall, pale, Byronic. A beautiful and sensual Dracula. Director Dennis Rosa has a flawless command of movement and timing."
—Richard Eder, N.Y. Times

"**S**pectacular! This is ghoulish fun in the grand manner. Edward Gorey has designed soaring, spectacular settings. They present the production in giant size and lead it into a gothic dimension. Frank Langella, a premier American actor, is flamboyant, aristocratic and swashbuckling. This is a performance by a true leading man and it is a brilliant one. It is action indeed and theater on the super scale, pure escape and great fun!"
—Martin Gottfried, N.Y. Post

DRACULA IS

"**A** show that's the summit of sumptuosity. Take your teen-agers, take your friends, take yourself to see one of the most entertaining productions I have ever, ever, ever seen on the stage!"
—Gene Shalit, Today Show, NBC-TV

"**D**racula in the grand operatic manner with a tall, lean, majestic and handsomely unwholesome Frank Langella batting his way about as the King of the Vampires. He is superb. Thrills and laughs along the way-'Dracula' is a triumph of production."
—Douglas Watt, N.Y. Daily News

"**D**racula, beautiful and battier than ever is indeed a Gorey affair. A stunning, delicious treat for all. An enchanting and unique evening in the theatre. Welcome, beautiful and batty 'Dracula' and may you arise nightly to chill Broadway for a long time, matinees too!"
—William A. Raidy, Newhouse Newspapers

"**D**racula is so entertaining and stunning. Frank Langella is elegant and fascinating."
—Howard Kissel, Women's Wear Daily

"**Y**ou would be batty not to see 'Dracula'! It reaches a triumphant tumult of escapist entertainment!"
—William Glover, Associated Press

"**A** rare stylish treat. The cast is strong right up the line. Frank Langella gives a brilliant performance. Dennis Rosa's direction is wickedly well stylized!"
—Thor Eckert, Jr., Christian Science Monitor

"**D**racula is a cinch to be on Broadway for many months. It's a great show for kids as well as adults!"
—Hobe Morrison, Herald News

"**I**f ever a show had hit written all over it, this is it!"
—Jacques Le Sourd, Gannett Newspapers

"**D**racula is a chiller that has the power to frighten and delight. This delightful diversion is the best show in town!"
—Emory Lewis, The Record

"**D**racula is a howling success. This is the big one with Edward Gorey's haunting sets and costumes driving you bats at every turn. A scare-raising evening at the theater—great fun!"
—Bob Lape, ABC-TV

"**I** loved it! Frank Langella is a heavenly vampire and I would willingly offer him my neck. I'm a sucker for 'Dracula'!"
—Pia Lindstrom, NBC-TV

"**T**his is a 'Dracula' you can really sink your teeth into. It should run for another 500 years!"
—Pat Collins, CBS-TV

"**S**piffy staging with marvelous gothic scenery and costumes by Edward Gorey. Have fun! And the kids will love it!"
—Stewart Klein, WNEW-TV

"**A** delight! A must-see night of delightful terror, but get home before dawn."
—Jeffrey Lyons, WPIX-TV & CBS Radio

"**F**ly like a bat to the Martin Beck Theatre!" —Jim Lowe, WNBC

"**T**his Broadway production is everything it should be. Atmospheric, stylized and altogether good melodramatic fun. A respected and serious actor for so long, Frank Langella is spectacular. A classical performance as choreographed as it is acted. The entire cast is splendid!" —Alvin Klein, WNYC

"**A** delicious, dazzling 'Dracula'! Theatrical magic. The story is told with a truly wonderful sense of humor. Frank Langella's performance is unbeatable. I direct you to 'Dracula'!"
—Kevin Kelly, Boston Globe

"**N**ow listen, you've got to go to the Martin Beck Theatre if you are anywhere within New York because 'Dracula' is one of the most perfect evenings I've ever had in the theater and Frank Langella is simply divine as the Transylvanian count. This is a dazzlingly, delicious wonderful night in the theater!"
—Liz Smith, N.Y. Daily News

SPECTACULAR!

"Dracula lives! The count is back in high style. Broadway audiences are assured of an evening of high-class fun. This is no lurid draught of blood, but a fine rosé – dry, slightly chilled, amusingly intoxicating. Frank Langella's 'Dracula' is a Transylvanian Prince Charming, a Byronic hero with a fatal flaw for blood. Never has the Count had such balletic grace or vampirism seemed more enticing." —David Ansen, Newsweek Magazine

"A delightful romp for sophisticates, children and vampire elitists. A solid boost for fun. In the person of Frank Langella as a demonic force from the nether world, there is lust but also a doomed lyrical romanticism. His 'Dracula' is no flittering bat but the noblest prince of darkness – the fallen Lucifer. For him this is a role of roles!" —T. E. Kalem, Time Magazine

"Grisly festivities at the Martin Beck. 'Dracula' is charming. Frank Langella plays with suave menace. To all the members of the cast, my thanks for making me laugh before shuddering." —Brendan Gill, The New Yorker

"An elegant production of nightmarish beauty. A seductive 'Dracula' to haunt your maddest dreams!" —Marilyn Stasio, Cue Magazine

"I went bats over 'Dracula'!" —Earl Wilson, N.Y. Post

JUJAMCYN THEATERS
ELIZABETH IRELAND McCANN   JOHN WULP   VICTOR LURIE
NELLE NUGENT   MAX WEITZENHOFFER
present

FRANK LANGELLA
in
DRACULA

Dramatized by HAMILTON DEANE and JOHN L. BALDERSTON
from Bram Stoker's world famous novel, "Dracula"
with

ALAN COATES   JEROME DEMPSEY   DILLON EVANS
BAXTER HARRIS   RICHARD KAVANAUGH
GRETCHEN OEHLER   ANN SACHS

Scenery and Costumes designed by
EDWARD GOREY

Scenery supervised by   Costumes supervised by   Lighting designed by
LYNN PECKTAL   JOHN DAVID RIDGE   ROGER MORGAN
Directed by
DENNIS ROSA

SEATS NOW AT BOX OFFICE & BY MAIL

PRICES: Tues. thru Fri. Evgs: Orch. $15; Front Mezz. $15; Rear Mezz. $12.9. Sat. Evgs: Orch. $16.50; Front Mezz. $16.50; Rear Mezz. $13.50, 10. Wed. Mats: Orch. 12; Front Mezz. $12; Rear Mezz. $9, 6. Sat. and Sun. Mats. 6 Hol. Mats. Nov. 24 6 25: Orch. $13.50; Front Mezz. $13.50; Rear Mezz. $10.50, 7.50. Evgs. Tues. thru Sat. 8. Mats. Wed. & Sat. at 2. Sun. at 3. Please enclose a stamped, self-addressed envelope with your check or money order. List alternate dates.

SPECIAL HOLIDAY MATINEES NOV. 24 at 3 P.M.: NOV. 25 at 2 P.M.
CHARGIT: (212) 239-7177. Charge seats with all major credit cards, daily incl. Sunday.
GROUP SALES BOX OFFICE: (212) 354-1032 or Toll Free (800) 223-7565
Tickets also available at all TICKETRON Outlets: (212) 977-9020.

MARTIN BECK THEATRE
302 West 45th Street, New York, N.Y. 10036 / 246-6363

Dracula. I've been fascinated with Dracula from the time I read the book in high school, to the fact that I was born one day before Halloween and have 13 letters in my last name. As a result, I find Halloween to be the most wonderful of holidays because it's all about mystical things, pumpkins and Sleepy Hollow and the like. So, when the show came along, I absolutely had to do it because he's my favorite character.

Illustrations are from DRACULA: A Toy Theatre. *The sets and costumes by Edward Gorey for the Broadway production of the play. Courtesy the Edward Gorey Charitable Trust*

Dracula and a bite out of Broadway

Over the centuries, Count Dracula has worn all manner of fashionable capes and flashed a mouthful of molars of all shapes.

The original count was actually a prince and scary didn't begin to tell the story. He was a fright, yet very much alive. Vlad Tepes, better known as "Vlad the Impaler", was the ruler of Wallachia, a section of Romania, in the 15th century where his favorite method of killing his enemies was to impale them on wooden poles. His reign of carnage—his army once massacred 30,000 people in one day—earned him the nickname "Dracula," meaning "son of the dragon."

He wasn't a vampire, but he certainly had a taste for blood. Once, when representatives from the Turkish Sultan refused to remove their turbans in Vlad's presence, he ordered the turbans nailed to their heads. Dracula's namesake met a fitting ending, though. After being captured by the Turks in 1476, he was decapitated and his head was displayed on a stake. Vlad's loathsome legend was kept alive by books describing his acts of cruelty and were among the first bestsellers in the German-speaking territories.

Author Bram Stoker ratcheted up readers' blood pressures even more with his 1897 novel titled *Dracula*. The fictional Dracula was a vampire masking as a count in a castle somewhere deep among the dense, dark forests and winding roads of Transylvania. The stage was set when Jonathan Harker, a young English lawyer who was sent to Transylvania to finalize a transfer of real estate in England to the count, arrived at the castle in pitch darkness to the accompaniment of howling wolves.

A pale, gaunt man, Count Dracula puts Harker's neck squarely in play as the main course of the plot when he lunges at his guest in "demoniac fury" after seeing that Harker had cut himself shaving. Harker soon deduces that Dracula requires human blood to survive, but he is then assailed by three seductive female vampires and is soon near death. Meanwhile, Dracula leaves the castle with 50 mysterious boxes, earth bound for England, where his lower and upper bite become focused first on Lucy Westenra, the best friend of Jonathan's worried fiancée Mina Murray, and later Murray herself.

There is not enough garlic in existence to save Lucy from Dracula's clutches. Nor Mina, for that matter, although they survive in the end. Ultimately it takes a gang of six, including some of the men who loved Lucy and Jonathan (who has returned from near death), to cut off Dracula's head and stick a sword through his heart.

Although the reviewers raved about it, Stoker did not capitalize on his work, which has been assigned to many literary genres over time including vampire literature, horror fiction, the gothic novel and invasion literature. At one point he claimed he got the idea for Dracula from a nightmare about a vampire king rising from his grave caused by eating too much crab meat. Stoker died a poor man in 1912, about 12 years before Dracula once again rose from the dead, this time on the stage and featuring Hungarian actor Bela Lugosi in his first major English-speaking role.

The stage play was written by Hamilton Deane in 1924 and revised three years later for Broadway by John Balderston at the urging of producer Horace Liveright. In the revised story, Abraham Van Helsing investigates the mysterious illness of the young woman, Lucy Seward, with the help of her father and fiancé, and discovers that she is the victim of Count Dracula, a vampire whose thirst for blood was without end.

A stake to the heart could never keep a good vampire down and so it was that Lugosi returned in 1931 to play Count Dracula in the movie, which found a frightened but willing audience that, having no clue as to the psychological makeup of the villainous vampire, cheered on the herculean efforts of a team of mere mortals who banded together to slay a supernatural force.

Dracula was on the loose again in 1957, wearing killer fangs and played by Christopher Lee in the film *The Horror of Dracula*. It was an international hit and Lee redefined Dracula for a new-age audience.

The *London Telegraph* wrote, "Max Schreck's Nosferatu was an ugly rat; Bela Lugosi was a slice of Transylvania ham." But when Lee first appeared in *Dracula* (1958) he was dark and sexy. Here was a vampire you wouldn't mind getting bitten by, although the sight of a cross could bring out the animal in him. Lee's Dracula swung from gentleman to animal as quickly as he could put his red contacts in. And as the sixties swung on, the character represented an archaic evil.

The 1958 *Dracula* was a cinematic shock. Hitherto, vamp films were restrained and dialogue heavy. Terence Fisher, the gifted Hammer director, rebooted the theme with gushing blood, white teeth and a count who could swing about on chandeliers. Many reviewers were unimpressed: 'Dreary and inept' (*Sunday Dispatch*); 'It fails to live up to the grandeur of its theme' (*The People*).

The public, however, loved it. Aside from the promise of sex and violence, it conformed to the dramatic good vs. evil showdown of the Cold War era. Lee's sensuality was subversive in that it hinted that women might quite like having their neck chewed on by a stud. But, in the end, Van Helsing won with the power of God and a sharpened stick. Max Weitzenhoffer was born one day before Halloween, sometimes called Devil's Night, which could explain why he was drawn to bats and werewolves as a child. Or it could have been all those afternoons at the Liberty Theatre

in Oklahoma City watching horror movies—*Dracula*, *Frankenstein*, *Bride of Frankenstein*, *The Mummy*. But vampires did more than make him cringe in his seat. "There were several things about them that interested me," Max said. "To me, they were very tragic horror figures in that they are doomed to a lifetime of something they didn't want to do until they got to be a vampire. I mean, they aren't a mummy that has been resurrected or a monster being built. They were initially a human being that has been transformed into someone with everlasting life as long as they get blood. They are not figures of horror; they're more figures of tragic consequences."

In 1977 Weitzenhoffer was dealing with a few personal demons of his own. For one, the art gallery had stopped being fun and, more importantly, it was becoming less profitable. He also was not thrilled with the direction modern art was taking and his interaction with artists and customers was not compensating for the losses.

The adrenalin rush that came with *Sleuth* also was fading, almost obliterated by his participation in *Tickles by Tucholsky*, an off-Broadway cabaret show, and the 1976 failure of the musical revival *Going Up*, which was Weitzenhoffer's first effort as a lead producer. The play was about a young man who pretends to be an airplane pilot to impress a girl and was based on a Louis A. Hirsch-Otto Harbach musical from 1917, which had been adapted from James Montgomery's play *The Aviator*.

To put it simply, *Going Up* never got off the ground and was closed after six weeks at the John Golden Theatre on Broadway. "On opening night, the whole orchestra was filled with people who had not come to see the show," Max said. "The cast was young and inexperienced, and their performance was a disaster."

His partner was Norman Stephens, the husband of Max's wife's best friend and a Princeton University graduate who eventually achieved success in Hollywood producing television movies and miniseries. As Weitzenhoffer and Stephens tried to wrap their heads around what went wrong with *Going Up*, the conversation eventually turned to something more positive—new shows—which is when Stephens mentioned that his friend John Wulp was interested in reviving the play *Dracula* on Broadway.

In 1973, Wulp had staged a new version of the play with the Nantucket Stage Company in Nantucket, MA, and had asked Edward Gorey, an illustrator known for his macabre, surrealist imagery, to design sets and costumes. For *Dracula*, Gorey, who had never worked in theatre before, created a mostly black-and-white design accented with bold splashes of red.

A self-taught artist born in Chicago, Illinois, Gorey had produced 40 volumes of drawings generally accompanied by austere, whimsically sadistic texts that read like minuscule versions of Gothic novels. An anthology incorporating 15 of his small-format works was published in 1972. Entitled *Amphigorey*, it won critical acclaim and was enormously popular.

Dracula and a bite out of Broadway

Weitzenhoffer saw *Dracula*, which incorporated some of Gorey's touches, for the first time at Goodspeed Opera House in East Haddam, Connecticutt, and knew immediately he wanted to take it to Broadway. Interestingly, the production that was to replace *Dracula* at the Goodspeed was a musical, *Annie*. "I asked Michael Price, the director of the Goodspeed Opera House, if I should take time to see it," Max explained. "He said it wasn't worth looking at. Both shows opened on Broadway at the same time, and it should be obvious to everyone that I made a very bad decision."

But it was Gorey's concept more than Max's own fascination with vampires that sold Weitzenhoffer on partnering with Wulp and fellow investors William L. McKnight of the Jujamcyn Corporation, Elizabeth Ireland McCann, Nelle Nugent and Victor Lorie in a production that was capitalized at $360,000. "Edward Gorey came up with the idea of all the sets being in black and white and basically the same for the costumes," Max said. "It was a three-act play, and in each set, there was something that was red, a red rose. Otherwise, the show was totally black and white. That was the pitch. Nobody had ever seen anything like that on Broadway."

The play also had the good fortune of having a talented director in Dennis Rosa, who dispensed with the unnecessary history lesson detailing every little aspect of Dracula's after-dark activity and where all the bodies were buried. "The script had to be edited to remove everything that took away from the initial story of the vampire . . . of Dracula and Lucy and love and loss . . . of the sexual nature of Dracula," Weitzenhoffer said.

Weitzenhoffer's vision was inspired by the 1927 Broadway show where Bela Lugosi's portrayal had women in the audience passing out over what amounted to one hunk of a vampire. Equal to the task, Weitzenhoffer's Dracula was as seductive as the giant thunderheads out west, which swirl and flash their way across the endless horizon until they are suddenly upon you and it's too late to run. Then again, most of the women who saw Lugosi had no intention of running. "The first thing that came to me to do in casting was to find a vampire that would be sexually attractive to women in the audience," Max recalled. "Not like the Hammer movies that were dripping with blood, but somebody that was really good looking and sexual in nature."

Calling Frank Langella.

Born in Bayonne, NJ, in 1938, Langella was a classic stage actor, although he had only made one previous appearance on Broadway when he was cast as Count Dracula. Nonetheless, it was a memorable one as Langella had already won a Tony Award for Best Featured Actor as well as a Drama Desk Award for his role in *Seascape*.

His New York stage career began with the leading role in the off-Broadway revival of *The Immoralist*. Subsequent roles in Robert Lowell's *The Old Glory-Benito Cereno*, *The White Devil* and *Good Day* earned him three Obie Awards, and for his portrayal of Will Shakespeare in William Gibson's *A Cry of Players* for the Repertory Theatre of Lincoln Center, he received another Drama Desk Award. Langella's motion picture career began with *Diary of a Mad Housewife*, earning him the National Society of Film Critics Award. Beyond New York his theatrical repertoire at the time included leading roles in more than 50 productions in major regional theatres.

Langella had yet to prove himself as a dynamic leading man on Broadway, where it matters most, but he was clearly the man for the part, starting with his size and stature. And when Langella goes to Lucy's bedroom in the second act to seduce her, revealing plenty of his chest, the sexual nature of that conquest was not lost on anyone in the audience. What also sold Weitzenhoffer on Frank was a slight quiver his eyes would sometimes make in the middle of an important scene. "It made him far more interesting on stage," Max explained.

The other players included Alan Coates, a member of Great Britain's National Theatre and the Royal Shakespeare Company, as Jonathan Harker; Jerome Dempsey, who made his Broadway debut in *West Side Story*, as Van Helsing; Dillon Evans, who was noted for his classic performances on stage in London's West End as well as his work on film, as Dillon Evans; Baxter Harris, who was fresh off a Broadway role in *A Texas Trilogy*, as Butterworth; Richard Kavanaugh, who had performed leading roles with several repertory companies in the States, as R.M. Renfield; Gretchen Oehler, a Chicago native who attended the Goodman School of Drama, as Miss Wells; and Ann Sachs, a graduate of the Carnegie Mellon Drama Department, as Miss Lucy. "The cast is strong right up the line," wrote Thor Eckert, Jr. of the *Christian Science Monitor*.

Langella initially balked at playing Count Dracula on the stage, taking two months to make up his mind to do the part before Weitzenhoffer and Wulp finally assured him the show would be done with style, dignity and integrity, exactly what Langella had in mind.

"I see the play as a love story, with Dracula very much in love with Lucy, so I insisted on no fangs, no red eyes, no hollow cheeks," he told Judy Klemesrud of *The New York Times*. "He is not a ghoul, not a ghost. I saw him more as a Byronic hero."

Klemesrud described Langella's performance this way: "He swoops onto the stage of the Martin Beck Theatre, a tall, lean figure swirling a red-lined black velvet cape dramatically around his shoulders. His expressive brown eyes are wide-eyed and wary as they take in the scene, his skin pasty white, his voice as deep and velvet as Gregory Peck's. Swoop. Swirl. Swirl. Swoop. Rolling eyes. Conspiratorial glance. Evil grin. He is half serious, half camp. Offered sherry, he politely refuses, saying, 'No, thank you, I never drink (pause) wine,' What he prefers, obviously, is to sink his teeth into a really good neck. He is Frank Langella as 'Dracula,' Broadway's favorite vampire."

The audience came to see Dracula, and it was plain that they could count

Dracula and a bite out of Broadway

on the Count, who did so much with the precious little time he had on stage—only 17 minutes out of a two-hour play. Weitzenhoffer also believes Langella had a lot of help from other members of the cast and the entire production team, which showed a very collaborative nature given that Gorey walked off the set in a dispute over where to hang painted ivy outside of the proscenium (arch) and never came back. In the end, Max said success was achieved by putting pieces together that nobody thought would work.

This stroke of genius or luck—call it what you will—didn't end with Gorey's brilliant concept for a black-and-white set or by opting for Langella instead of a bigger name. There were plenty of other turning points in the production, starting with flying bats. It took a special effects expert from the Ringling Brothers Barnum and Bailey Circus to figure out how to fly bats mechanically across the stage without suffering a number of crash landings. And then there was Rosa, who came up with the idea of underlying music from the movie *Exodus* during the dramatic chase scene in the third act when the good guys are looking for Dracula's tomb in order to drive a stake through his heart. "The idea of having music come up in this way was common in the movies but not in the theatre," Weitzenhoffer explained.

Rosa, also an actor and a writer, was already being called a "Renaissance Man" by the press by the time he directed *Dracula* because of his success with adaptations in both the theatre and opera. While Gorey's inspired set design brought new meaning to a centuries-old character, it was Rosa who brought substance to *Dracula*.

"Romance, mystery, and death, these are the themes upon which I have based my work on *Dracula*," Rosa wrote. "I wished to present the evil of Dracula as intriguing, seductive and, yes, even humorous, a thoroughly appealing figure. Why? In this play of good vs. evil, why stack the deck so heavily on the side of Dracula so that we feel how difficult it is to resist him? Reason, religion, the civilizing laws of society are all on the side of goodness; we know they must win out in the end; we know they will. But unless we feel that we too could be tempted to give ourselves over to the evil of Dracula, just for the safely brief time we sit in the theatre, we will not feel relief or the sense of salvation when goodness triumphs, not a moment too soon, at the end."

The package was coming together. There were Gorey's spectacular sets, including the touch of red in each of the three acts. Then there was Langella's captivating time on stage, made even more powerful by Rosa's brilliant direction. But two essential details still needed to be addressed. One, the production was still about $180,000 short to be fully capitalized. Two, the show needed the right theatre. Those are often the hard parts to solve on Broadway, but again fate, luck, happenstance, talent, whatever name you want to give it, was on their side.

"We had an indication from one of the Shubert Theatre managers, who had seen an earlier version of *Dracula* at Nantucket, that the Shubert really liked the concept of doing the show," Weitzenhoffer said. "I didn't really know Bernie at that time, and the longer we were in his office that day to pitch it to him, the more he kept shuffling papers on his desk and the more nervous I got. Later, I learned that was one of his techniques to control the situation.

"Anyway, John Wulp said to him, 'Well, Warren Caro (a Shubert Theatre executive) said he liked it.' I think Bernie answered that by saying that Warren didn't really like it, "DID you?" and then he looked at Warren, who had no choice but to say that Bernie was right."

Wulp then tried to switch the conversation to the all-black and white scenery design, to which Jacobs showed his disdain: "Nobody cares about scenery."

Crystal clear on the fact they would get neither money nor a stage from the Shubert, Weitzenhoffer and Wulp turned to Sam Schwartz of the Jujamcyn Corporation which owned theatres in New York, Boston and Philadelphia. Schwartz liked the idea and helped capitalize the production, as well as offering to house the show at the Martin Beck, which opened on W. 45th Street in New York City in 1924 and was considered the most opulent theatre of its time.

The final check that green-lighted the show came from New Jersey investor Victor Lorie, a bit of a mystery man to Weitzenhoffer, who had been recruited by Nelle Nugent and Elizabeth McCann, both of whom were first-time Broadway producers.

The show was previewed at The Colonel in Boston, where it did very well. "I was sitting behind a group of young women on opening night and in the second act, when Langella came out with his shirt open and walked toward Lucy's bed, one of the women said, 'Boy, I'd like to have him suck my neck.' That's when I knew we were home free with the sexual angle," Weitzenhoffer said. The show opened on Broadway on Oct. 20, 1977, as the perfect build-up to Halloween. Save for one reviewer, the critics weighed in with glowing prose straight from the crypt:

> *"A complete delight. An extravaganza of horror; funny, charming and with a happy touch of serious authenticity. It has style, wit, chic. Frank Langella's 'Dracula' is exquisitely conceived and dashingly executed. Vastly entertaining, it gives Broadway a shot in the arm. A veritable blood transfusion."*
>
> —— CLIVE BARNES

Dracula and a bite out of Broadway

136

"Elegant, taut and visually stunning with a powerful, bone-shaking ending. Frank Langella's stunning figure as Dracula: tall, pale Byronic. A beautiful and sensual Dracula. Director Dennis Rosa has a flawless command of movement and timing."

— RICHARD ELDER, *N.Y. Times*

"Spectacular? This is ghoulish fun in the grand manner. Edward Gorey has designed soaring, spectacular settings. They present the production in giant size and lead it into a gothic dimension. Frank Langella, a premier actor, is flamboyant, aristocratic and swashbuckling. This is a performance by a true leading man and it is a brilliant one. It is action indeed and theatre on the super scale, pure escape and great fun."

— MARTIN GOTTFRIED, *N.Y. Post*

"Dracula in the grand operatic manner with a tall, lean, majestic and handsomely unwholesome Frank Langella batting his way about as the King of Vampires. He is superb. Thrills and laughs along the way—Dracula is a triumph of production."

— DOUGLAS WATT, *N.Y. Daily News*

"Now listen, you've got to go to the Martin Beck Theatre if you are anywhere within New York because Dracula is one of the most perfect endings I've ever had in the theatre and Frank Langella is simply divine as the Transylvanian count. This is a dazzlingly, delicious wonderful night in the theatre."

— LIZ SMITH, *N.Y. Daily News*

With reviews like that, it was no wonder that Langella's salary went from about $3,000 a week to $30,000 overnight. In all, Dracula totaled 925 performances on Broadway and made ten times its capitalization. However, there were a few hiccups. A Time Magazine cover featuring Langella was scrubbed at the last minute because of breaking news somewhere else in the world. And Langella posed his own sort of challenge with his backstage demands, whether it was insistence that the path between the stage and his dressing room needed to be painted between a matinee and evening performance or his calls to the box office between acts to complain about the temperature on stage.

"I happened to be there one night and answered the phone because the general manager was out," Max said. "Frank said it was hot and the audi-

Dracula and a bite out of Broadway

ence was rattling their programs and that was annoying him. I didn't do anything about it, but he called back in the middle of the second act and said, 'Where's the air conditioning?' So, I run around the theatre and find the stagehands playing cards, which is what they usually did, and tell them to go turn the air conditioning on. Again, Frank calls again. This time he says, 'It's much better.'"

Other than having to deal with Langella's idiosyncrasies, Weitzenhoffer had no complaints as *Dracula* proved to be a model of artistic and box office success. "Even Ann Roth's costume pieces fit together perfectly," Max said. "But the reason so many shows don't work is because when you start piecing them together, somewhere by the time you get to the end of it, you find that the pieces you picked don't quite fit and then something always goes wrong. There are times in shows when you can change the cast and you bring in a new star or a new actor and then adjust for them. You might change something on tour, but once you get your notices, you pretty well have to live with what you have."

In this case, Weitzenhoffer had a big hit. The taste of the champagne didn't linger long, however, not with those two damn words, "What's next?" hovering over Broadway like a skyscraper's shadow.

Broadway. The "It" factor is simple here, too, because Broadway is the "It." There is nothing anywhere else like it, other than the West End in London. Broadway is the epitome of quality. There's nothing better in theatre than what appears on a Broadway or West End stage. I mean it's the accumulation of the greatest talent we have available at the time to create something breathtaking.

Henri Rousseau, Street in the Suburbs.
Oil on canvas, c. 1896

A man is a man and
his word is his word

e prefers his art in the abstract, often with an Egyptian flair, but when it comes to doing business, Max Weitzenhoffer is pure vanilla. A handshake will suffice; he learned this the hard way. The price was a pittance, really, because in his estimation, the lesson he learned has served him well in the theatre, where the orchestra pit often doubles as a snake pit every time vanity and greed raise their ugly heads. In a profession full of uncertainty, his peers know they can count on Weitzenhoffer to do what he says he will do.

As is the case with many things in his life, he got on the right path by accident. And not surprisingly, his mother was involved. The year was 1966, around the time Clara was still buying pictures from Europe. Somehow Max found himself engaged in a search for art for his mother when he ran across a painting he liked that was owned by the highly reputable Dutch art dealer E. J. van Wisselingh, from whom his mother had purchased her Van Gogh.

"I saw a photograph of the picture and I sent Mr. van Wisselingh a note, or maybe a telegram, telling him we would buy it for $10,000," Max recounted. "Then, I thought to myself, why would I buy something I haven't seen?"

So Max sent another telegram saying he wanted to see the painting before purchasing it. The response caught him off guard because van Wisselingh appeared to be much more concerned about honoring a gentleman's agreement than he was in making a sale. "If you would have asked me to see it first, I would have sent it to you, but you told me you were going to buy it," van Wisselingh said. He went on to add a few words that have stuck with Weitzenhoffer ever since: "He told me that they have a saying in Holland that is translated this way and that I've always quoted: 'A man is a man and word is a word.' van Wisselingh told me that I didn't have to buy the painting but that I should remember that when you give somebody your word that you are going to do something, you do it."

Weitzenhoffer now owns both the painting, which hangs in the Fred Jones Jr. Museum of Art, and the philosophy that came with it. "That's why in the business deals I've had with Lloyd Webber or anybody in my business, anybody will tell you, when I say something or agree to something, cast something or say I'm going to do it, it's a handshake; it's not a contract, and my word is good."

A man is a man and
his word is his word

143

The half-a-million dollars he wired to Lloyd Webber and Really Useful to get *Phantom of the Opera* rolling came without any piece of paper to verify the exchange of money. Weitzenhoffer simply sent the money and forgot about it. That's the way he has operated with almost every show he has produced. "Stiffing people is sometimes the nature of the theatre business, whether the show is a flop or not. But when Weitzenhoffer and Frank Milton flopped with *Harold and Maude* and were $300,000 over budget when they closed, Max sold some property in Norman and his partner sold his apartment in Olympic Tower to pay off everybody they owed. "I have never left anybody unpaid. And I've never done business with anybody that doesn't have the same philosophy," he said.

That wasn't his only hard and fast rule. Another one was to not blindly pursue your fascination for a show over a cliff because then everybody loses. "You have to psychologically say to yourself, 'I am not going to put a lot of people out of work.' And I must accept the fact that it's my fault if a show doesn't work," Max says. "It's not because this actor didn't do his job or is the press agent's fault. The reality is, if the audience doesn't like the goddamn thing, they won't go and if they don't like it, it's your fault because you put it up there."

Weitzenhoffer has invested in productions that fulfilled every expectation to the extent that he, too, was ready to jump out of his seat on opening night. But there also have been times when he wanted to crawl under it. "I've done things where I go to the first rehearsal, the first read-through, and I came home and put myself in bed. And my wife came home and said, 'Why are you in bed?' Because I've just been through the first read-through and I've hired the wrong people and it's going to be terrible and I can't stop it. It's a snowball; I've already paid everybody and there's nothing I can do about it. Part of this creative process one goes through is, you must realize that not everything you create is any good, and if it's not any good, you must own that, too. Nobody's done it to you, you've hired every single person that is now doing it."

Two of his biggest disappointments were the revivals of *American Buffalo* in 2008 and *A Little Night Music* in 2009. Unfortunately, Weitzenhoffer determined *American Buffalo* was doomed from the moment he saw it at the first preview in New York City. Nica Burns, who has co-produced many shows with him, called Max later that night to see whether she should come to opening night.

"I said, 'Don't come over; it's terrible.'"

Burns came anyway, and what a waste of time and money that was. Opening night proved to be hideous, as reflected by the overnight notices. At the next morning's marketing meeting, the show's general partner and manager were standing in front of the group offering ways to redirect the advertising campaign and save the show, when Weitzenhoffer and Burns started laughing.

A man is a man and his word is his word

"We said to them, 'Close it. You have $600,000 you can return to investors, so close it." They said, 'Oh, no, we're not going to do that.' So, we left the room, and that's when we decided we would never go to New York again."

As for *A Little Night Music,* it performed well when it featured Catherine Zeta-Jones, who had a lot of Hollywood box office success to her credit. When her contract ended, Weitzenhoffer and Burns wanted to close the show, having already turned a healthy profit. "But our partners, and there were more of them than us, wanted to replace her with Bernadette Peters and, unfortunately, she didn't sell," Max said.

It is the producer who must pull the plug, but on the flip side, that doesn't mean producers will get credit for backing a hit. "The press only wants to talk to the playwright who wrote the big hit, the director and the cast," he insisted. The producer's role is to use his vision and mind to correctly assemble all the parts, create a positive force and then fix what goes wrong if that's possible. In that regard, Weitzenhoffer's intentions were as good as his handshake. What counts most is whether the producer knows what in the heck he's looking at. "My strength is I know if it's going to sell or not," Max said.

In the end, however, every "hit" needs an "It." For example, when Max's wife Fran was researching her book on the Havemeyer's, she had some interaction with their grandson who told her about meeting film editor Watson Webb, whose great claim was editing the film *Kiss of Death,* starring Victor Mature, in which Richard Widmark had a small part as a gangster who was part psychopath. The most famous scene in the movie is where Widmark pushes a woman in a wheelchair down the stairs and then laughs. "When he was editing the film, Watson Webb sees this bit and he goes to director Henry Hathaway and says, 'Have a look at this. This guy is something really special.'" Weitzenhoffer said once Hathaway looked closer, much of the film was reshot to emphasize Widmark's role. That one scene and the "It" factor he demonstrated helped make him a leading man.

Unfortunately, live theatre is not designed for making sweeping changes on the fly and is far less forgiving than the big screen, making it doubly important to employ another rule of thumb—The Logan Principle. The Logan Principle is very simple, according to Max. When director Josh Logan was doing *Mr. Roberts* out of town, it didn't work; it was flopping, and Logan couldn't figure out what was wrong with it until he went and looked at all the plays Maxwell Anderson wrote. When he started reading them, Logan discovered that all the hits had one thing in common. Weitzenhoffer calls it "The Journey," and his primary goal as a producer is to take his audience on a journey, from the moment the ticket holder sits down in their seat until the end of the show. If the audience hasn't been taken on a satisfactory trip, the show will not work—ever.

Richard Widmark

A man is a man and his word is his word

The theory, he says, applies to *Mister Roberts* and every other production.

In the ending of *Mister Roberts*, Lt. Douglas Roberts' former shipmates on the World War II Navy cargo ship *Reluctant* got a letter saying he had been killed in combat. But the play's journey was not complete until the moment when Ensign Pulver, who was regularly maligned by the captain, threw the unpopular ship captain's replacement palm tree overboard. It was Roberts who dispatched the Lt. Commander Morton's first palm tree in protest to his hostile treatment of the crew and now Ensign Pulver was taking his place as the one to stand up to the captain. "You're very moved at the end and that makes the whole thing work," Max said. In contrast, in the first version of the script, Mister Roberts was successful in getting transferred off the ship and went on to successfully complete his dream of fighting in a big battle. That wasn't a satisfactory journey to the audience, according to Weitzenhoffer.

"It's the same thing with musicals, even in the simple-minded ones, such as *Annie Get Your Gun*. She goes and shoots all those stupid things and then has a love affair with Frank Butler; he gets mad and leaves and she's such a good shot but at the end she misses," Weitzenhoffer said by way of comparison. "She deliberately is forced to miss and so at the end they get together and that's the twist. The journey has been completed for her; she's now back with him in the end."

One of his most profound disappointments came with one of his favorite productions, *Three Guys Naked from the Waist Down*. He calls it a great show that didn't pass the Logan Test. One of the few good reviews the show received nailed it perfectly, saying the first act was wonderful, that the second act was XYZ but that in the third act everyone was wondering what they should do next. At the end of the second act, Three Guys wound up being three characters standing around, a point that was painfully driven home to the audience.

Weitzenhoffer has produced 17 shows on Broadway, four off Broadway and another 24 on the West End in London. He has also been involved in the production of many others. Stopping short of there being a formula, here's how he learned to put on a show:

For starters, he finds something he really likes, which means something that moves him and gets him excited to see it on stage. Weitzenhoffer accomplishes that by either seeing a straight play or musical at a regional theatre that he could potentially bring to New York or London, or by being drawn to a script that lands on his desk courtesy of a playwright's agent or the postal service. Weitzenhoffer seems to prefer the former. "I'm not quite a master of knowing what I'm reading," he says. "I mean I know what it's about, but sometimes its potential passes me by, like that time Morty gave me *Same Time, Next Year* and I thought it was awful. I came home and told Fran I had been given the script and that it was nothing more than a TV show. I did get my revenge indirectly, mentally, because

A man is a man and his word is his word

I never went to see it the whole three years running in New York. When it was revived about 10 years later in New York—I think it was *The New York Times*—said that they don't understand why it was just so successful, because it looks like a TV show. I took that to my wife and said, "SEE, SEE, I was right and have been vindicated; somebody else saw it the same way!"

Once he opts for a script, the next priority is to team with someone who thinks the same way he does, usually a director, because the relationship between the producer and director is of paramount importance. Sometimes Weitzenhoffer will seek out a director to gauge what he or she has percolating. Other times he will start with a playwright to discuss potential ideas or he might commission a play to be written. And if you get lucky like producer Manny Azenberg, you discover Neil Simon on the ball field. The two met when they played softball with Robert Redford in 1962, and Azenberg and Simon went on to produce *The Sunshine Boys*, *The Good Doctor*, *God's Favorite*, *They're Playing Our Song*, *Brighton Beach Memoirs* and *The Goodbye Girls*, among others. In a newspaper article, Azenberg offered that he was not a deep thinker or a writer, although he said he recognized a good idea when he saw one. He thought what a producer should be noted for was the ability to create an atmosphere that was genuinely comfortable in order for the best creative work to take place. "You try to keep peace, because there are so many disparate groups within the theatre," he said.

It's always a trick to find a director who specializes in the type of production the producer has in mind. "All directors have their own unique style and bring their own vision to a production," Max said. "It's their signature, and a producer is smart to understand that going in."

The leap from playwright to director is a critical one because the conversation then shifts to determining what kind of physical production will be involved, which then throws the set designer into the equation. And set designers are all different, too. Plus if it's a big musical, that will involve the input of a lighting director and a composer and a choreographer, as well as a book writer, who will have their own artistic styles. "That's what I mean about fitting the pieces together," Weitzenhoffer said.

The feel of a juggler. The patience of a kindergarten teacher. A backbone of steel—well, at least something that doesn't bend like a slinky. No, there are no special skills required to be a producer. Once the creative team is in place and the number of characters and scenes have been determined along with the scenery, costumes and musical score, and when a stage manager has been hired and a theatre has been secured, it all comes down to one thing: How much is this going to cost me? Metaphorically, the yardstick used to measure that aspect of the show is getting longer all the time. It's almost out of sight, compared to 30 years ago. It's also a variable that must factor in four weeks of rehearsal and then address the question of whether the show is taken out of town for

A man is a man and his word is his word

previews or whether previews are held on Broadway, which, depending on the show's popularity, could dip into the reserves or add to the profits.

If the producer still insists on pouring other people's money (and maybe some of his own) into what could very well be as costly as a dry hole in the oil patch, he or she then must hire a lawyer. "The lawyer has to prepare the offering documents to meet the approval of the government and the Securities Exchange Commission," Weitzenhoffer said. "The lawyers are all a bunch of nasty individuals because those documents are boilerplate. Every show has the same outline for a document as every other show except you have to do the arithmetic differently according to what the show's going to cost and then the lawyer will charge you some gigantic fee for all the time he spends on it, which is no time whatsoever, because he just prints out what he had from the last show and just fills in the number, sends you a bill for $50,000 or $60,000. I mean, that's the way it works."

At that point, the producer is looking for help—an equal partner, preferably—to help share the pain or gain and to attract investors. Nowadays it's not unusual for the names of 20 investors to appear above the title of a show because it takes a minimum of $5–10 million to bankroll a musical on Broadway. Long before the laws on investing tightened up and production costs skyrocketed, Weitzenhoffer could round up six investors at $30,000 each to finance a typical show. "You would basically call the people you knew, normal regular theatrical investors, people around town that always invested in shows that you knew through opening night parties and things like that," Weitzenhoffer said. Today, the typical investment units are $25,000, $50,000 and $100,000, which goes beyond the realm of play money.

Rule one for Weitzenhoffer is to never ask anybody to put money into a show in which he doesn't personally invest. It might not be an equal amount, but the point is he wants his backers to feel that he has their back, as well as his own. "When you present the show to potential investors, you have to show them based on the budget you've got in that theatre that Show X is going into theatre Y, and that said theatre can gross X amount of money at capacity. Then you have in your budget what you call the running costs which lays out weekly what you will make if the theatre is operating at capacity or 50 percent. That gives you an idea of how long it will take to recoup our money. In the big musicals, it could take you as long as 50 weeks or more to get back what you spent, which is a lousy investment. Normally, with a big musical in the old days, it was 26 weeks. That's what you want, 26 weeks to get your money back, and with plays you want to get your money out in almost the same amount of time because you generally gross less money."

"From Weitzenhoffer's perspective, picking the right theatre should be treated like an art because every theatre in New York and London wears its own fragrance and it's up to the producer to know which one will go best with his show.

There's a lot to consider—the theatre's size, its personality, the way it sets up. It's vital to have the right show in the right theatre because a theatre should feel like home to the audience, and if it's uncomfortable in its home, the audience will tend to dislike the show, as well.

When it hosted *Dracula,* the Martin Beck was considered to be jinxed because it sat on the wrong side of 8th Avenue, a notion Weitzenhoffer found amusing. What the Martin Beck had going for it in Max's mind was that it was very Gothic on the inside, Dracula's kind of place to be sure. The Beck also had one other advantage because it had a balcony overhanging the orchestra seats, which meant every seat in the house could be sold at full price. "It was a one-price house, which meant, hypothetically, your gross would be gigantic in a 1,400- seat theatre or so," Weitzenhoffer said.

The reverse was true at the Palace Theatre, where *The Will Rogers Follies* played. It had a third balcony with several restricted view seats that could not be sold, which meant the producers had to reduce revenue expectations. "You put in your mind, 'If I go to that theatre I'm not going to be able to have maximum gross because I can't sell those seats in the third balcony.' I know Morty Gottlieb had a show called *Things That Go Bump in the Night* and he told me that when he had a third balcony he used to advertise all the seats for a dollar and he still couldn't sell them."

The choice of *when* to open equals, if not exceeds, *where* to open in importance. For his part, Max always yearned for springtime on Broadway. Fall was good in that it overlapped Thanksgiving and the holiday season. But then along came January and February, which could send an average show into a chill and all but freeze out a mediocre one.

"What you want to do is open in April or so, because you want to be playing during the Tony Awards show (which are held in June) because if your play closes before the Tonys, your chances of getting a nomination are not very good," Weitzenhoffer volunteered. "And secondly, you get additional publicity if you are nominated, and it helps you if you take the show on tour."

That was certainly the case with *Pump Boys and Dinettes*, a 1982 musical revue created by Mark Hardwick and Jim Wann, who both worked at The Cattleman restaurant in New York City playing country music five nights a week while the waitresses catered to businessmen in classic western saloon girl attire.

Critics considered the pair's dramatization of their experiences at the restaurant to be a small triumph for ensemble playing and *Pump Boys* earned three Tony Award nominations, including Best Musical. The outcome could have gone much differently if not for Weitzenhoffer and his "Tony Theory."

Weitzenhoffer's producing career was in a slump when Liz Shepherd

A man is a man and his word is his word

walked into the office and told him about an audition of a show she had just seen. Shepherd was a University of Oklahoma drama major who had worked part-time for Max at his art gallery. She knew theatre and was always looking for new productions.

"I have a show I think you should get involved in," she told him.

After seeing an audition for himself, Weitzenhoffer decided to back the low-budget show along with Dodger Productions, Warner Brothers and two other investors. Additional backers could not be found, so the five backers each put up $20,000 and decided to open the show off Broadway at the 100-seat Colonnades in Greenwich Village.

"Well, it just took off. It got great reviews and we didn't have enough space for everybody to see it, so that's when I made, probably, my first intelligent decision," Weitzenhoffer said. "At a production meeting, I opened with how 1982 was going to be a terrible year for musicals and that we should open at a theatre that was eligible to be nominated for the Tony Awards." Weitzenhoffer's partners, meanwhile, wanted to move it to a 400-seat theatre off Broadway to increase revenue potential.

Weitzenhoffer won that round, and the show was moved to what was then called the Princess Theatre, which was considered a Tony eligible venue, in the Latin Quarter. It had not been in service for a while, but the owners set up the theatre to meet the needs for the *Pump Boys*, which included tables of six as a cabaret might have where the customers could drink alcohol while they saw the show.

"We each had to put up our share of the move," he said. "I think my cost was $50,000. I knew we had a giant hit, so it was no big deal. I went to the bank and borrowed my share of the money."

His hunch panned out. *Pump Boys* sold out night after night and got its Tony nomination for Best Musical, which earned it national television exposure, another year on Broadway and a national tour. "We knew we weren't going to win, but we were the first big number of the evening, which is also what you want when the Tony Awards are televised," Max said.

Pump Boys got Weitzenhoffer back on his game.

The importance of when to open a show also is driven home by the critics because at that point their perspective carries tremendous weight. "I'm telling you that even picking the night you open is critical," Weitzen-hoffer said.

The overnight reviews, particularly what Frank Rich of *The New York Times* had to say, could make or break a show. If you thought you had a big hit and want a great reveal, you open on Thursday night, which would get you an overnight review in the Times and a second review by a different critic in the *Times'* Sunday edition. If you thought the critics might skewer your show, you opened on Friday because the *Times'* Saturday edition was not as well read.

"You know, it's not like getting Mickey Rooney and Judy Garland and saying, 'Let's put on a show in a barn somewhere.' It's just a lot of money at risk," Max said. "You have investors who are counting on your expertise to deliver what you promised them, and then you have the situation where you basically have outlined everything negative that you can think of before doing the show. But something is going to go wrong that you never experienced before and now you're going to have to deal with it, but you don't know what it is, and it may be like it was with *Harold and Maude* when the star decides to quit."

Things might move along swimmingly until the phone rings and there's a problem on the other end. "You don't know what it is, so you can't prepare for it. In *The Will Rogers Follies*, the opening number is so spectacular that Willa Kim couldn't get her costumes finished in time for the first preview. So everybody had to come out wearing blankets, and we had to tell the audience in advance that we were short on costumes so there will be people wearing blankets."

It might have put a damper on the evening, but based on what came next, *The Will Rogers Follies* proved to be anything but a wet blanket.

*A man is a man and
his word is his word*

Fran. She didn't just adjust to my eclectic likes and dislikes. She bought into all of them and became an integral part of everything that was going on in my life. Her ability to connect with people, to entertain, to make intellectual small talk in New York where that is an art. Everyone told me what a fantastic person she was, and they were right.

Will Rogers

Where there's a Will . . .

The world certainly admires a man who can twirl a lariat and talk at the same time. At least, Florenz Ziegfeld Jr. sure saw a lot of star potential for someone with such skills. And more than 70 years later, so did modern-era showman Max Weitzenhoffer.

It often takes one to know one, and when it came to William Penn Adair "Will" Rogers, no one could entertain folks better than he could. Ziegfeld quickly latched on to him, making the Oklahoma cowboy the featured star in the *Ziegfeld Follies* on Broadway in 1916. Not to be outdone, Weitzenhoffer, who has always been partial to both cowboys and musical revivals, reintroduced stage audiences to the man with a rope, a grin and a quip in the 1991 Broadway production *The Will Rogers Follies*.

By frontier standards, Weitzenhoffer and Rogers practically grew up over the hill from each other. Weitzenhoffer was born in 1939 along Oklahoma's geographical divide, not far from the Chisholm Trail where the tumbleweeds gather in the crevices of the red rock canyon walls and along mostly dry creek beds. Rogers grew up about 150 miles to the northeast and 60 years earlier on his parents' ranch along the banks of the Verdigris River in a lusher setting, known as Indian Territory when he was a boy.

In truth, the forces of nature—a temperamental soil and the whistle of the wind—were about all they shared because Rogers died in an Alaskan plane crash alongside fellow Oklahoman and famous aviator Wiley Post four years before Weitzenhoffer was even born. Max couldn't miss the fact that the bright, shiny new movie house in Oklahoma City carried Will Rogers' name. And he knew that Rogers had starred in a lot of silent films and half as many talkies. But compared to the epic westerns that director John Ford was filming in Monument Valley, AZ, Rogers' crude cinematic efforts felt as creaky as old age. Although Weitzenhoffer knew of the museum that had opened in Rogers' hometown of Claremore, Oklahoma, he had never visited it, or else he would have been far more impressed with the cowboy, humorist, vaudeville performer, newspaper columnist, radio personality, movie actor and all-around philosopher rolled into one. Clearly, 'multi-talented' did not do Will justice.

Will Rogers is remembered as a man for the times, a bridge between the Old West and a new age of global conquest for America. He made people feel comfortable with his 'aw-shucks' manner, and they laughed long and loud at his jokes. More importantly, he made them think about society and building a more caring country with his ability to capture what the nation was thinking and using satire as a sword in defense of decency and fairness. He poked fun at the rich and powerful—politicians, gangsters, prohibition, big government in general—and he got away with it because the rich folks laughed just as hard as the plain folks. He could say more with fewer words than any songwriter not named Woody Guthrie.

For example:

"Even if you are on the right track, you'll get run over if you just sit there."

"Never miss a good chance to shut up."

"If there are no dogs in Heaven, then when I die I want to go where they went."

"Too many people spend money they haven't earned, to buy things they don't want, to impress people that they don't like."

"Everything is funny as long as it is happening to somebody else."

"There are two theories to arguing with a woman. Neither works."

"All I know is just what I read in the papers, and that's an alibi for my ignorance."

—— WILL ROGERS

After roping and riding his way to fame, Rogers discovered audiences also appreciated what he had to say. They also liked the fact that he was as free as the open range, unencumbered by barbed wire or snobbery. By 1916, he was no longer the "Ropin' Fool." He had transformed himself into the "Talkin' Fool" after he became a featured star in the *Follies*, where he left President Woodrow Wilson in stitches with his off-the-cuff, witty commentary on current events.

For all he had to offer posterity, Rogers was close to being nothing more than a museum piece until producer Pierre Cossette brought a script about Will Rogers to the late Eric Shephard, the agent for director Tommy Tune, who said, "You've gotta have a better look. We should get Peter Stone." (A noted screenplay writer at the time.)

As reported by John Harris in *TheaterWeek*, Stone turned them down, explaining he didn't find biographies interesting. "You either have to lie, and that doesn't serve history very well, or you end up with something strange but not very compelling," Stone said. Tune had similar feelings. "Rogers' life is not musical, and he didn't have a highly conflicted life—he became a great man and died tragically."

But both men could not get the idea out of their head, particularly Tune, a Texan who identified with Rogers' cowboy ways. And when he learned that Rogers got his big break when Ziegfeld signed him up for the *Follies*, Tune knew they had the makings of a new musical, an endeavor that also included Cy Coleman (music) and Betty Comden and Adolph Green (lyrics). "We thought that setting his biography in the *Ziegfeld Follies* would give the material the theatricality that his real life lacked," Tune said. "Then we had to find out what the *Ziegfeld Follies* were because we all had these vague mystical ideas about them."

Tune's lasting image of the *Follies* was cemented in his childhood when a neighbor who had seen it in person described her experience. She said the curtain opened to reveal a great big bunch of grapes. Each grape popped open and within every one was a beautiful girl. When all the grapes had opened, a big grape leaf fell across the stage.

It sounded wondrous to Tune the child, but it was now 1991, and he knew that kind of naïveté would not work on Broadway. He wanted something more vibrant than a period piece. As told by Harris, Tune incorporated the elements of the *Follies*—production numbers, sketches, monologues and acts—and used them as building blocks to tell Will Rogers' story.

"We had never used all of those things and fused them into telling about one man's life on this earth," Tune said. "We really are making it up as we go along, with nothing to fall back on."

The original concept to do a stage show based on the life of Will Rogers came from Cossette, a television producer best known at the time for producing the Grammy Awards show. He had made a deal with the Rogers family in 1982 to obtain the rights to the memoir of Betty Rogers, Will's wife. He then put together his creative team which included Stone the book writer, Coleman, Comden and Green, and raised $200,000 at his first backers' audition in 1989, well short of the $6.25 million projected budget.

James Nederlander, president of the Nederlander Organization, and his partner Stewart Lane eventually pledged $1 million, provided the show was slotted into the Gershwin Theatre, which was difficult to book because of its cavernous size. But Tune, who was both the director and choreographer, objected, leaving the fate of the show in limbo.

That's where Weitzenhoffer entered the picture. It started with a phone call from Nederlander and Lane inviting him to join them and the production's creative team at the Tavern on the Green. They played a hunch that Will and Max were two Okies who were made for each other. "They said they were going to bring a piano and talk about the show, sing some of the songs, describe the scenes," Max said. It was better orchestrated than that because Cossette had flown in Keith Carradine for the last-ditch effort.

Weitzenhoffer decided to attend, but he did not exactly run to get there. While Rogers was Oklahoma's Favorite Son, the Okie connection in and of itself was not enough to energize Weitzenhoffer, who saw Rogers as a character study. And character studies didn't interest him as the basis for a show.

Max also wasn't feeling decisive about much of anything at that moment in time. While *Dracula* had transformed him overnight into a producer of note, the nine Broadway shows he had subsequently produced, six on and three off the big stage, had left him with bruises. For example, *Harold and*

Maude had cost him $60,000 of his own money and a lot of disappointment. While that play didn't send him into hiding, it made Max unsure what to do next.

He finally opted to produce a comedy, *The Good Parts*, off Broadway in 1982, but it wasn't funny enough. *Pump Boys and Dinettes* earned a Tony Award nomination and, besides lifting his spirits, Max learned a lot of do's and don'ts that come with taking a production on tour.

Then it was a step back with *Three Guys Naked from the Waist Down*, followed by the unexpected failure of *Song and Dance*, which Weitzenhoffer still calls his favorite musical, despite what the audience thought. From 1985-1989, he continued his up-and-down run with *Blood Knot, Burn This, Road to Mecca* and *Largely New York*. Of the four, *Burn This*, a play by Lanford Wilson, played to critical acclaim on Broadway for more than a year. It dealt with gay identity and relationships at the height of the AIDS epidemic and was noted for both its subject matter and the performances of the cast. Joan Allen won a Tony for Best Actress in a Play; Lou Liberatore won the Theatre World Award and was nominated for a Tony, while John Malkovich was up for a Drama Desk Award for Outstanding Actor in a Play.

In addition, Weitzenhoffer backed such successful ventures as *Equus, The Elephant Man, Mass Appeal* and *Les Misérables*. But he turned down a chance to invest in *Big River*, saying he knew it would be a hit but he wasn't certain it would be a money-maker. He liked *Jelly's Last Jam*, too, with Gregory Hines, but worried what would happen to it when Hines left the show, a fear instilled in him by Bernadette Peters' departure from *Song and Dance*.

By that point, Weitzenhoffer had earned membership in what James B. Freydberg called "The Big 8"—a small band of deep-pocketed individuals who continued to invest in the theatre for a living. Among the names, according to Bruce Weber of the *New York Times*, were Martin Richards, Terry-Allen Kramer, Kenneth D. Greenblat, Roger Horchow, Roger Berlind, and Weitzenhoffer. Every producer on Broadway knew who they were, which is why the Big 8 generally heard about every project that was in the works long before corporate backers, who were becoming more essential on Broadway.

Big musicals were particularly risky, which was the other reason Weitzenhoffer was not immediately roped and tied by the prospect of producing *The Will Rogers Follies*. Audiences were demanding spectacular sets and sophisticated pyrotechnical effects. When rising labor costs and the need to pay a big-name star to sell tickets were thrown into the budget, it might take a year's worth of performances for a show to break even. The risk of losing money betting on a Broadway show was so great that even horse racing was considered to be a safer wager than the theatre.

Thus, Weitzenhoffer wasn't exactly feeling the love the day he left Tavern on the Green, Aug. 9, 1990. Then a week later he got a tape in the mail that had been made of the meeting, highlighting some of the tunes and Carradine's talents. He held it in his hand and almost wasn't going to plop it into the VHS player to show his wife Fran.

But it wasn't fear of failure that gave him pause. Fran was dying. The cancer they thought she had beaten ten years earlier had returned with a vengeance, spreading to her bones and other organs.

"I really wasn't in the mood to do anything," Max said.

At her insistence, he finally showed her the tape.

"What are you going to do?" she asked.

"Well, I'm going to forget it," Max responded.

There was a pause.

"No, you have to do it," Fran finally said. "You have to do it."

With that, Weitzenhoffer picked up the telephone and called Pierre to work out the details. He would put $500,000 of his own money into the $6.25 million game, along with Cossette, who came up with more than $1 million of his own money. Nederlander, Lane and Morty Richards also contributed. Japan Satellite Broadcasting, a communications conglomerate that wanted to be able to film the show for its pay-per-view network, ensured the show would go on with a $2 million commitment.

Fran died on March 10, 1991. She had climbed to the top of her field as an art historian and seemed to make a lasting impression on everyone everywhere she went. Max was lost without her, but as is required, the show went on. One saving grace for Weitzenhoffer was the beauty of the production that arrived as a complete package, a stunning package at that, from the creative team to the cast to the stage crew. It was almost unheard of on Broadway to have an all-star team in place from conception. "Nobody needed to be hired. It was just a question of going to the first day of rehearsal," Weitzenhoffer said.

Carradine was the final puzzle piece. Tune told *TheaterWeek* that he couldn't imagine the quirky, contemporary performer playing Will Rogers. "I wanted a regular guy plunked into the middle of all the glamour of the *Ziegfeld Follies*," Tune said. "I thought the contrast would be welcome. That's what made it work with the real Will Rogers, someone just like my dad spinning his yarns.

"And the thought of my father being the star of the *Ziegfeld Follies* . . . But Keith came in and auditioned for us. I was just taken. After he left, Betty, Adolph, Cy, Peter and I clasped hands in the middle of the Imperial Theatre and said, 'We've found our Will.' And then we started shaping the show knowing it was going to be for Keith."

The only risk that came with that decision was that Carradine did not qualify as a box office draw the way singer and actor John Denver (who was initially considered for the part) did. Carradine won an Academy Award for Best Original Song (*Nashville*) and had appeared in numerous roles on film and television, along with some minor stage work with his famous father

Keith Carradine and the new Ziiegfeld Girls in The Will Rogers Follies.

John Carradine. Yet he could not be expected to fill the house by merely lending his name to the marquee.

Even without a big star to lead the way, Weitzenhoff had the visceral feeling he usually gets when he likes what he sees on stage. "I think the most important thing about the theatre has nothing to do with raising money and doing all the build-up," he said. "It has to do with one thing—does it grab you? Does what they are doing on stage grab you while you are watching it? What's going on inside your gut is what tells you whether it is any good or not.

"For example, Nica (Burns) and I did a show in London. I can't even remember what it was, and when we went to the final dress rehearsal, we looked at each other and said, 'This is terrible.' It had nothing to do with the fact that it wasn't well-produced or well-acted or whatever. It simply didn't work."

It wasn't until the full orchestra assembled in the large rehearsal hall and played the whole score from the show that Weitzenhoffer knew what they had on their hands. Nonetheless, that did not automatically make for smooth

Where there's a Will . . .

160

sailing. For example, the costumes had to be hand-made and were late arriving. There was too much scenery for the stage. There were complaints that the chaps the chorus girls wore left too much of their buttocks exposed, which in the end probably helped ticket sales as part of the marketing campaign involved featuring them in a giant billboard in Times Square. There were objections to the show's portrayal of Native Americans and the lack of black cast members. There was a Visa problem pertaining to the Australian trick roper who had been imported to give a taste of what the original Will Rogers could do. And there were complaints from a critic that the theatre owners were selling tickets with obstructed views. Weitzenhoffer said the claim was erroneous but to avoid bad publicity, a section of the balcony was blocked off, which cut into the gate.

There were two instances leading up to opening night where Weitzenhoffer assumes he made a difference. The first involved the show's ending. The plot came without much suspense as much of world already knew that Rogers perished in an airplane crash in Alaska. For the finale, the script called for everyone on stage to be dressed in black-and-gray costumes with newsprint headlines marking Rogers' death plastered on them. It was moving, to be sure, but moving as in how a funeral procession moves, which is opposite of what Weitzenhoffer wanted the audience to feel when it left the theatre.

He made his feelings known at the production meeting. "This is a musical comedy," he volunteered. "How are you going to end the show in a death scene with everybody in gray and black?"

He went on: "Then, there's always a reprise of the 11 o'clock number (a show-stopping number) after the curtain call to get the audience going, so how is the cast going to get back into those dazzling costumes they had in the big opening number for the show?"

Everyone agreed, and in the new ending there was nothing glum about Will's farewell when a member in the audience, on cue, screams out, "Let's go flying," and Rogers answers, "Not yet."

A more problematic issue arose during the previews at the Palace when it was calculated that the show would require a $700,000 infusion to keep the doors open through the Tony Awards, where it was expected to win several honors and another boost in popularity.

Cossette came up with an unpopular solution. He wanted to close the show early to avoid spending more money. His partners in the room at the time—Weitzenhoffer, Richards and Stewart—were stunned. "We could tell from looking at the audience that the show was going to work," Max said. "How big a hit, we didn't have any idea. But we told Pierre, 'All right, we're going to put up the money and you go away. Just leave and give us the whole show.'"

Cossette decided to stay. The four men anted up the additional $700,000 and by the time Will Rogers finally took his last curtain call, the musical had grossed about $57 million, although it took two years for them to even recoup half of their investment.

The Will Rogers Follies opened on May 1, 1991, to glowing reviews, save for one from The New York Times. Its success was made more remarkable by the fact that it was based on the life of a man from an obscure place whose specialty was defusing conflict rather than creating it, and who died long before most present-day theatre-goers were born. "In a way, you were introducing people to almost a fictional character, and I believe that's the way most people saw it," Max said. "But the show made a wonderful connection between the audience and the real Will Rogers. I think one of the most amazing things about him was that while his humor was based on making fun of somebody in a funny way, nothing Will Rogers ever said was nasty, pointed or unpleasant."

The producers' decision whether to keep the show going turned out to be a no-brainer because luck was on their side. The other big musical on Broadway that year was Miss Saigon, which was based on Giacomo Puccini's opera Madame Butterfly; only this time the doomed romance shifted war zones to Saigon at the height of the Vietnam War. Instead of a marriage between an American lieutenant and a geisha, it featured a romance between a U.S. GI and a South Vietnamese bar girl with the tragic underpinnings of a war gone wrong.

For all its splendor and political overtones, Miss Saigon didn't offer what mattered most in the spring of 1991, a reason to wave the flag. The U.S., with the help of its allies, had just defeated Iraq in Gulf War I and the country was rejoicing that it took so little time to achieve victory with so few casualties. "There was an enormous military parade in New York, which had not been done in years," Weitzenhoffer emphasized. "Regardless of how one feels now, there was a very big plus feeling about our country at that time. One night, Gen. Norman Schwarzkopf Jr., the U.S. general who led the Coalition Forces, came to the theatre and the whole audience stood up and started cheering. That's not typical New York, but it was during that period."

The country was on a high and it didn't want to be brought down by Miss Saigon. Then again, the Follies had more than flag-waving on its side. It benefitted from the ultimate team effort, winning Tonys for Best Musical, Best Musical Score, Best Direction of a Musical, Best Choreography, Best Costume Design, and Best Lighting Design. It also won Drama Desk awards for Outstanding Choreography and Outstanding Music.

"I think the best part about the Tony Awards, like the Olivier Awards, is that they are given by your peers," Weitzenhoffer said. "It's not 'he deserves it this time.' It's the fact that you did something that was better than what anybody else did at that moment. You have a lot of ups and downs in the theatre, and when I get it right, I am good at what I do."

Once the show opened to the applause of both New York theatre-goers and Okies there to see Will, the fact that he had a spiritual connection with Will Rogers was not lost on Weitzenhoffer. Some say the grand land that is Oklahoma is also cursed. The creeks swell only to dry up when your back is turned. The soil won't grow anything but hard times, and the blast furnace that constantly sweeps across the plains can put an OK man down. But Will Rogers showed the world that Oklahoma was really OK with his infectious spirit, sense of humor, and his sense of justice. Weitzenhoffer was proud to bring Will Rogers back to Broadway. It's not every day that you get to produce a big hit about somebody from your own backyard, a possibility that did not escape Fran Weitzenhoffer when she told her husband to do the show.

"The most amazing thing for me is the relationship I developed with Joe Carter of the Will Rogers Museum and what he taught me about Will Rogers," Weitzenhoffer said. "At the time of his death, Will was the highest-paid entertainer in America. Think about it."

It was a grand way to honor Oklahoma's Favorite Son, for sure. The curtain rose to the sound of an airplane in the distance, followed by skywriting that spelled out "Ziegfeld presents The Will Rogers Follies." Then there was silence, time dedicated to remembering that both Rogers and Post died in a plane crash. But as described by Oklahoman writer Robert Haught, the audience was soon humming along with songs such as *Never Met a Man I Didn't Like*, *Will-A-Mania* and *Give a Man Enough Rope*.

Carter, who assisted with research and went through early run-throughs of the show, attested to its historical accuracy. "The musical *Oklahoma!* was fantastic," he said. "What this show does beyond that is carry you into the life of Will Rogers and makes people aware of all the fine virtues of Oklahomans."

When the show went on tour, naturally it stopped in Oklahoma City. Carradine sang the National Anthem at the Oklahoma-Nebraska football game in Norman. "I think the Sooners lost," Weitzenhoffer said.

Maybe it was time to put Max in the game.

Where there's a Will . . .

If you want the show to go on, Max Weitzenhoffer claims the following rule should always apply: When you replace a star, you better replace him or her with a bigger star.

That was true when Richard Burton took over for Anthony Hopkins in *Equus* and boosted ticket sales. And that's how Marla Maples, with a little encouragement from Donald Trump, her boyfriend at the time, made it to Broadway as Ziegfeld's favorite chorus girl in *The Will Rogers Follies*.

Maples wasn't a star in the traditional sense. She became famous for having the looks to steal another woman's husband, an awkward fact that didn't escape Weitzenhoffer and other members of the production team when they held auditions to replace Susan Anton, who had been a big hit in the show.

"We had heard that Marla Maples, who at the time was Trump's significant other, had an interest in being in the show and wanted to audition," Weitzenhoffer said. "There were about eight of us sitting in the Palace Theatre when she walked in with Mr. Trump. I can't remember what she did on stage in the audition—I think she had a bouncing ball of some sort. Well, she did her thing, and Donald took her away."

Afterward, Betty Condon, Tommy Tune, Komen and Weitzenhoffer and a few others gathered in a small room at the theatre to discuss their options.

"Right off, Adolph Green said, 'Well, she can't sing, and she can't act, and she can't dance, but she will sell tickets.' So, we hired her. It was as simple as that, and there was no dispute. And if you want to know the truth, we got great publicity, and she was pretty good."

Here's how *The New York Times* reported Maples' August 3, 1992 opening night performance:

In the opening minutes of her opening night, Marla Maples rose slowly from the orchestra pit, a Venus rising on a hydraulic lift, and shimmered in gold cowboy boots, gold hot pants, gold cowboy hat and gold hair. As applause rippled around her, Ms. Maples sang, twirled a giant branding iron, strutted and skipped across the stage, smiled and wiggled her nearly naked behind. She didn't trip, and she dropped neither the iron nor a note.

"Her pants are too tight,' Harrison J. Goldin, whispered to his wife, Diana.

"That's the idea,"she replied.

Mr. Goldin, the former city comptroller and a financial consultant who has advised some of Mr. Trump's creditors, was one of some 300 friends and business associates who last night accepted the real-estate developer's invitation to attend the stage debut of his fiancée, Marla Maples, in The Will Rogers Follies.

But there were hundreds of other members of the audience who had no personal connection to the famous couple, and who actually paid to see the Broadway show—or at least the woman who has graced the pages of tabloid newspapers for months. "I wanted to see the woman who stole Ivana Trump's husband,"said Dale Canner, who explained she had seen the show with the original cast.

That was the idea. Publicity Boost.

Even in the play, Will Rogers's wife, played by Nancy Ringham, turns to Ziegfeld's Favorite and says wonderingly, "How did you get this part?" The audience cracked up and Ms. Maples rolled her eyes knowingly at the line that was restored specifically for her.

And Donald J. Trump, who held a Western theme party for 500 in the grand ballroom of the Plaza Hotel after the show, made no secret of his relationship with the blonde newcomer. There were moments last night, in fact, that seemed more in keeping with Donald Trump's Folly. When they arrived together at the Plaza, Mr. Trump had his arm around Ms. Maples and wore the proud, possessive look of a William Randolph Hearst presiding at the debut of his young protege, Marion Davies.

Ms. Maples confided to half a dozen television cameras that Mr. Trump had come backstage after the first act "and it gave me that plug to get back in there."

Earlier at the theatre, Mr. Trump greeted such guests as LaToya Jackson, Mike Wallace, Frank and Kathie Lee Gifford, the real-estate developer Lewis Rudin, Maury Povich and Keith Carradine, the actor who originated the lead role, now played by Mac Davis. Mr. Trump, who received more than 200 complimentary tickets, beamed as if he had written, directed and financed the show.

"'Citizen Kane' is my all-time favorite movie," he confided happily. "I know, I know," he said, mulling over whether there was any resemblance between his support of Ms. Maples' career and the plot of the movie based on Hearst's romance. Finally, he said, "I see no analogy between the two." He added that his role in persuading his friend Pierre Cossette, the show's producer, to hire Ms. Maples, had been small. "You can have all the friends you want," Mr. Trump said. "If they don't think the person is a terrific talent, no way can they be at the Palace Theatre."

"It's amazing what a little money can do," Irene Calabrese said rather acidly, as she stood nearby, watching Mr. Trump bask in the warm glow of television camera lights. Ms. Calabrese had come to see her daughter, Maria, a chorus girl. But by the time she spotted Kathie Lee Gifford, Mrs. Calabrese had whipped out her camera. "For a person who is not affected," she said ruefully, "I'm having a very good time."

It was not quite Ms. Maples' first time on stage. The show's creators had sneaked her into a few performances, both to get publicity pictures, and to give Ms. Maples a chance on stage. "I love her voice," said Tommy Tune, who coached her dancing. "I've never worked with a media star before."

Once the house lights were dimmed, and Ms. Maples began trotting up and down stage, Mr. Trump left his seat and paced at the end of the house. "She has been under a lot of pressure lately," he had said earlier, "but she's showing she can handle pressure. She's got a lot of talent; I'm not surprised."

In that, he was almost alone. As Dale Canner put it when explaining how she persuaded her husband to see the show a second time, "I'll bet you anything she can't act."

"Everyone is waiting for slips," Mr. Povich said, "but there aren't any. I think she is living up to the role."

Or, as Peter Stone, who wrote the book, said, "The show is just playing its Trump card."

The Follies, with some help from Maples, went on to play another year on Broadway before closing on September 5, 1993. Maples and Trump married in December of the same year. It ended with their separation in 1997.

Ayako. There is something about the Japanese in general that is fascinating to me. Part of it is their history, the culture, the theatre. Even their architecture has had tremendous influence on Western world. And from the first time I saw her, I saw a mystical quality in her. I can't tell you why because it's impossible to describe why you are totally attracted to someone. It's just a feeling that grows from there.

Home again

Nothing beats the rhythm of a big Broadway musical and the rolling thunder of a chorus line. Except, possibly, for places in Manhattan like Lobel's Meat Market on 82th Street and Madison Avenue.

Throughout the 1980s, Fran Weitzenhoffer often shopped at Lobel's for a main course for dinner. One day she dropped in to buy a cooked chicken.

Stanley, the butcher behind the counter, matter-of-factly proclaimed, "Well, we don't have any more chickens because this gentleman just bought my last two."

"Well, my husband is going to be very disappointed because he was counting on chicken tonight," Fran replied.

At that point the stranger standing next to her interjected, "Allow me to give you one of my chickens." He handed her a chicken, turned to Stanley and said, "And take care of my usual order." Then he was out the door.

A bit taken aback, Fran had a question for Stanley. "Who just gave me that chicken?"

"That was the Russian ambassador," he answered.

She couldn't stop there. "I don't want to be nosy, but what is his usual order?"

It was hard to say no to Fran, so Stanley finally blurted it out: "We don't tell anybody, but they buy $10,000 worth of steaks a month to send to the Kremlin."

That said almost everything you need to know about the unique flavor of the Big Apple for the 30 years Max Weitzenhoffer called it home. Almost every transaction had a subplot. Nothing was as simple as it seemed. Nothing moved in that town in those days that didn't have a beat to it.

When he first arrived in 1965, there were nothing but mom-and-pop stores on the Upper East Side. None were named Gucci's. There was a repair shop, a laundry, a shoe store, a bookstore and on and on. Among the rows of brownstones was a bar downstairs in at least one house on every block. You could grab a burger or get a steak and have a drink or two. Or maybe carve your name on a panel on the wall. Down in the Village, the comics would come out at night and laughter would be about the only thing that cut through the dense, smoky atmosphere. It was toxic, yet addictive.

Weitzenhoffer rented for a while before finally settling in at 77th and Madison Avenues where he purchased an apartment on the top floor of a 10-story building. He laughingly referred to it as 'the penthouse.' It had been built around the time of World War I when a lot of places had maid service, and in this building, all the maids' quarters and laundry operations were on the top floor. Eventually the quarters were converted into the apartment that Max lived in. The one drawback was that the only way to get to the top floor was to take the main elevator to the 9th floor and walk up one flight of stairs to his apartment. However, the view was more than worth it.

"It was a different life then. It was a big city, but you knew all the people you dealt with," he said.

He could walk his dog to the little supermarket where Pip would raise up, put his paws on the glass counter and eye all the meat in the case until the butcher would give him a snack.

There was plenty of wealth in that part of the city, but for the most part it was old money, which meant it was not to be flaunted. That's not to say money was not important because when it came to operating a business or owning a home, there were some Third World aspects to the big city that Max could do without. The bottom line was everybody had their hand out when it came to getting anything done.

"You had the underhanded stuff going on by everybody that worked in the city," Weitzenhoffer said. "Everybody that had to have anything done for you, you had to pay them off to obtain a building certificate. A building inspector wanted me to install giant fire doors between two open rooms in my art gallery."

The demand went away when Weitzenhoffer bought the inspector two tickets to the Bahamas. New York was known for its prize fights and its football Giants in the '80s, but all of the muscle wasn't in the ring or on the field. If you didn't pay, you didn't play anywhere in New York. "At least you could always go to Little Italy to have a meal and never have to worry that you're going to get hit in the head," Max said.

Sometimes tough guys with muscles were even appreciated in the sanctity of the theatre. When the last-minute investor in *Dracula* (without whose involvement there might not have been a show) invited a group of burly men wearing thick chains around their really thick necks, Weitzenhoffer did not bat an eye, so to speak.

But there was something else about New York that all the mouth-watering Italian food in Little Italy could not overcome. "One of the reasons I left New York, versus why I particularly am attached to London, is the fact that New York is historically a city that is constantly tearing itself down and rebuilding itself," Weitzenhoffer said. "It's not a negative, but New York City doesn't have a culture that goes back hundreds of years which has been totally maintained without movement. I mean, I had to think about it the other day when I was in a taxi in London going up to Covent Garden, where our office is, from where I've always lived over in Chelsea. I thought to myself, 'I'm on this street and I'm going by Buckingham Palace up the mall, and whatever, and going over here, and stopping off at a couple places that I like to stick my head in,' and I thought to myself, 'I've been doing this for 60 years, and it hasn't changed.'"

Home again

As with New York City, Weitzenhoffer had built something on Broadway and instinctively knew it could not last. Something had to change. The point was driven home to him in several ways.

First, he lost his wife.

Actor David Niven, whom Max greatly admired because he could maintain an air of sophistication while at the same time seeming to suppress a laugh, said in his best-selling memoir *The Moon's a Balloon* that he left Hollywood because it wasn't fun anymore. Max grew to feel the same way about New York after Fran died.

He also knew that the high of *The Will Rogers Follies* would not last forever. "It was one thing that my own mother told me she didn't like it, which is why I didn't invite her to the opening, but I also knew that what happens when you do a big musical like that, there comes a point when you know you're not ever going to do another one because times have changed."

Weitzenhoffer drove another stake in his romance with Broadway when he got involved in *Eating Raoul*, an off-Broadway production that was billed as a whacky musical comedy that was derived from the film by the same name, a black comedy that acquired a bit of an international cult following. The play focused on Paul and Mary Bland, two hapless squares and their quest for a piece of the American Dream through capitalism, sex, the strategic use of a frying pan and some tasteful cannibalism.

One critic called it indigestible, adding, "Perhaps inspired by *Sweeney Todd* and even that more modest *Little Shop of Horrors*, someone decided that *Eating Raoul* should be ripe for music. Perhaps it was—but not this time and not this music."

Weitzenhoffer was last on the list of producers, the primary place of blame if a show fails, and *Eating Raoul* only made it through 38 meals, err, performances.

His attitude toward New York also was affected by something beyond his control—death. After 25 years on Broadway, Max started losing his peers in the theatre. "You can talk about the setting sun, the meaning of it. Well, you start feeling it from your friends when a lot of them begin to shut down earlier than others. Your contemporaries in life begin disappearing and shutting down."

Ultimately, it was a matter of economics for Weitzenhoffer. Broadway angels—backers who put up money in a show and then got out of the way—had all but vanished, along with those with modest expectations of gain. And Weitzenhoffer was among the last of small band of deep-pocketed investors who were in the game to make a profit.

It was precarious times, indeed, if a big hit such as *The Will Rogers Follies* could barely turn a profit. It was the same for *Guys and Dolls*, hailed as a savior for Broadway when it opened in 1992. Ditto for *Jelly's Last Jam*, which won three Tonys but had trouble recouping its investors' money. Broadway was a long way removed from the days of plenty, such as *My Fair Lady* (1956), which cost $350,000 to stage and six weeks to recoup on its way to a 6-year run. Then there was *Annie,* which cost $1 million in 1977 and earned about $300 million. The shows simply got too expensive and the risks became too great.

So he went home. Just like that. Weitzenhoffer kept his apartment, but he said goodbye to Broadway. "It started as a real diversion because I had fallen, and I really didn't know what to do," he said. "I wasn't depressed. You aren't depressed until the train runs over you."

Home was not Oklahoma City, though. Norman, Oklahoma, was home, as close to the University of Oklahoma campus as he could get. As is typical of university towns, a lot of vibrancy was crammed into a confined space marked by narrow, tree-lined streets. The main campus was 32,000 strong now, about twice as large as when Max graduated in 1961, but the core was much the same. To the north there was Campus Corner, an area of bars, restaurants, coffee houses and retail shops where everybody eventually made their way. Part of the reason for that was because the southern end of campus for the most part remained a gaping hole, ripe for development, which ultimately came with the arrival of a new university president, David Boren. On the west side, the arts were more in vogue from the Fred Jones Jr. Museum of Art to the performing arts theatres along Elm Street. What mattered most, however, was that Mecca, as observed by an obscure sect of Oklahomans who wear lots of red attire, was still to the east and bigger than ever, not better, yet the football stadium and the scoreboard that had flashed many a Sooner victory remained the most visible symbol of achievement to which the university could point.

Weitzenhoffer had returned often to Oklahoma over the years mainly to take in a lot of football, which was an indication of his true priorities in life. His father had purchased him membership into the Touchdown Club when Max was only 10 years old and letting it lapse has never been under consideration. Football, after all, is played on a stage with tubas and drum majors in the orchestra pit, and if you are in Oklahoma, it plays to 80,000 people strong. "Everything sits inside of something. A football game is framed in a field a hundred yards long and so many yards wide," he said. "That's what you are looking at for three hours. That's the frame, just like a stage."

Oklahoma football remained about the only stable force in his life in 1992. *Eating Raoul* had soured him on the theatre. In fact, a whole decade would come and go before Weitzenhoffer would be tempted to back another Broadway show.

Furthermore, his relationship with his mother had not improved over time. She had continued to remind him that he made a mistake by not following his father and grandfather into the oil business, and he had to win his second Tony Award for *The Will Rogers Follies*, which earned him induction into the Oklahoma Hall of Fame, before she would acknowledge that Max's father would have been proud of him. Somehow, her admission still rang hollow to him.

"When I was a child, I heard my dad say to my mother that he didn't want me to work as hard as he did, but that's the way it worked out," he said. "I do work as hard as he did, but I do it in a way that I enjoy."

It's not always apparent if Weitzenhoffer is serious or not because his expression is often one of mischief. He can be charming when the conversation interests him, impatient when it doesn't. With his friends, he often aspires to be outrageous or politically incorrect, hoping to get a reaction. To strangers he might appear aloof, wearing a look only the rich can afford to have because they know they are never going to run out of money. It's not that he is void of emotion. He cried at his father's funeral and at Fran's memorial service. But he has learned to be guarded. He will still cry when he watches the ending of *The Field of Dreams* when Kevin Costner realizes that Shoeless Joe Jackson is his father. But when he does, he will turn away, so his son Owen won't see the tears.

He has an eye for talent both on and off the stage and appreciates and rewards loyalty. His business acumen is often underestimated because traditional corporate culture considers the theatre to be more of a frivolity than a business. The reality is he would probably have been more respected by business leaders if he had started a successful hamburger chain rather than produced hits on Broadway. "I realize that creativity isn't given the same level of respect in the business world as someone who has invented something or started a business," he said. "I'm not knocking them, but I'm saying that when you paint or write or act and that when you do something that affects a large number of people in a very moving way, that's a real statement."

His rather nonchalant approach to both work and play should not be mistaken for weakness because while he might not bear a grudge, he will find a way to get even if pushed too far. "I do have a side of me for revenge," he said.

The best example pertained to his Uncle Mark, his father's oldest brother. Mark hated Max's mother with a passion and the feeling was mutual, Max says. His father couldn't stand him, either. Perhaps it was said in jest, but before Max was born, Mark told Clara that he would give her $100 if the baby was a boy and a box of peanuts if it was a girl.

"Then one time, when he came to Oklahoma City on business, my father gave him his car to drive. "It had a stick shift and I guess he couldn't figure out how to get it out of third gear and when he brought it back, it was a disaster."

After his father's death, Max's mother wanted Max to be appointed to the board of directors of the Seminole Manufacturing Company, the family business the brothers had started in the 1920s. "Of course, Uncle Mark didn't want me on the board because he thought that would mean my mother would be hanging around," Max said.

It involved paying a sizable gift tax but it was worth it to his mother, who transferred all her stock to Max in hopes of getting him a seat on the board. "So I go to Mississippi with my father's lawyer, Vip Crowe, who was one of the greatest country lawyers ever, and we had a knock-down drag-out at the board meeting trying to get me on the board. Of course, I didn't have the votes because my uncle had control of the company."

It wasn't until his uncle died that Max got elected to the board. But the story didn't end there. "I didn't like my relatives and I didn't like the way they were running the company. I can't remember how it happened, but as they kept dying off, I kept buying their stock. When I controlled over 50 percent of the company, I did whatever the f--- I wanted. I fired my relatives from the board, sold part of the company and brought in new management and moved the company to Michigan."

Returning to Norman was just another episode in a mini-series because, as former University of Oklahoma official and longtime friend Tripp Hall has observed, Weitzenhoffer goes where his curiosity takes him, which is often from one show to another.

For example, when Max decided to sell his New York "penthouse" and hang out in his old college stomping grounds, no one assumed he could sit still for long.

It so happened that he was sitting at the kitchen table one night with two friends from Norman, U.S. District Judge Wayne Alley and his wife Marie, when he had a brainstorm. Alley, in and of himself, is a remarkable story, having served on the three-judge military panel that convicted First Lt. William L. Calley Jr. for his role in the My Lai killings during the Vietnam war and approved his sentence of 20 years of confinement and hard labor. Alley was later appointed to a new seat on the U.S. District Court in western Oklahoma by President Ronald Reagan. Weitzenhoffer and the Alleys became close while Fran was still alive, and after her death the Alleys' kitchen table was where he did a lot of his best thinking. It was there that the idea of starting a musical theatre school at OU emerged and that Max should make it happen along with his best friend at the time Greg Kunesh, who he met through mutual friends at OU, and set designer Raymond Larson and his wife Gloria. Although their friendship later dissolved over what Max described as philosophical differences, what Weitzenhoffer terms his biggest accomplishment in the theatre might not have happened without Kunesh, who had been replaced as dean of fine arts from the drama school, which made him available to take on the challenge with Max. In their view, the musical theatre school was to be a place where new musicals could evolve from scratch and where drama majors could get practical training for Broadway.

Home again

Is He Dead? *A stage
production at the A. Max
Weitzenhoffer School of
Musical Theatre.
Photo by Sandra Bent*

"What really came over me was that we should be teaching some students to go into musicals. Nobody was doing it except maybe the University of Michigan and Miami, but not very many," Weitzenhoffer explained.

It wasn't just the wine that was talking that night at the Alleys.

"I pitched it to the provost that we could get money back with our productions. He liked the idea and so did the dean," Max said. "Before that there was the school of drama and the school of dance, but musical theatre was always below that stuff."

From 1998–2000, Weitzenhoffer contributed $5 million to create the musical theatre program from scratch and threw in another $250,000 to convert what had been storage space into a 200-seat theatre where the musicals *The Great Unknown* and *Lily & Lily* had their world premieres. Prior to that, Weitzenhoffer used his connections to Broadway to create opportunities for OU to be a staging area for potential Broadway productions such as *Jack*, a 1995 musical built around the assassination of John F. Kennedy. While *Jack* didn't make it to Broadway, it helped put musicals on the map at the university.

In the beginning all the program possessed were two offices, one for Kunesh and one for Weitzenhoffer and his organ. They had to beg and borrow their way through the early years, whether it came to recruiting students to be on stage or in the crew for a new production or whether faculty members were needed to provide guidance. It was normal for Weitzenhoffer to scour sorority and fraternity talent shows for talent. "We went from being a program to being a department to being a school by cobbling it together," he said. "That's a pretty big deal because we were the first program to be elevated to department status since Dr. Cross left the university."

While it does come with a degree, what gratifies Weitzenhoffer more about the school he created is that it has put hundreds of its graduates to work in the theatre since its inception. "It's my biggest accomplishment," he said.

What Weitzenhoffer stressed then and what still might hold true today was that talent alone won't beat hard work in professional theatre. "When I was running the program, we had three quite talented young women who came to see us as they were graduating, and they were going to New York and wanted to talk about what's next. I was in my office with one of the other faculty members and I said, 'Okay, I'll tell you right now. You go into New York and there are some rules you must remember apart from the work ethic:

One: Don't get married because, frankly, it doesn't work. You'll find somebody who's not in the business and you'll have hours opposite of what theirs are and it doesn't work. If you're both in the business, it might not work because one of you is more successful than the other. If you have a baby, that doesn't work. All these things can work at a later point in your career, but these are things you need to get out of your mind.

"Two: As far as dating when you get to New York, you make every effort to go to every social function you can think of that is involved in the theatre, whether it's an opening night party or whatever, and you don't get involved with anybody unless they can help you. It's called networking. It will get you a job because the fact of the matter is when you get there, you're going to be faced with many people that are just as talented as you are, and they may be more clever at getting a job than you are but that's the name of the game.

"And three: Don't ever be late for auditions and always dress properly for the audition; you need to be very conscious of the people you're auditioning with and don't get on a personal basis with them. And if you're lucky enough to get a job, never, ever be late. I've been through so many auditions where somebody, even a star, would come up or a photograph of them comes up when we are discussing whom to hire, and the director or someone will say, 'We can't deal with this person; they come to rehearsal late; they're argumentative.' And once you are branded, you are finished."

Weitzenhoffer then alluded to a past graduate who had one of the leads in *No Strings*, for which Richard Rodgers wrote the words and music. The

Home again

student later told Weitzenhoffer that he was offered money to do a shaving commercial and was desperate for money, so he didn't shave for days because of that commercial. Then Richard Rodgers sent word down to the stage manager that the guy had to shave, but the young actor refused to do so. Rodgers got irritated with him and for several years, he never got any work because it was reported that he was difficult to work with.

"You can't f--- around with these people, which is why you have no idea how tough this business is," Weitzenhoffer said.

Not long ago he stood in the back of a classroom in the drama depart-

Home again

ment, near the door and out of the way, which is his style when it comes to public appearances. The room was filled with high school students from across the country, many of whom were accompanied by their parents. They were on campus that weekend to audition for a scholarship in the school of musical theatre. The program funds 14 full rides every year. This group had already survived the first round of auditions, which usually involves as many as 800 applicants, and their faces captured both the excitement and the apprehension of the moment as the pool ultimately would be winnowed down to a select few.

As he surveyed the room, Weitzenhoffer pictured himself back in time, a freshman at the University of Oklahoma who was every bit as drawn to the stage as the talented bunch of high school students sitting in front of him. The only difference was that he couldn't sing or dance, except when it came to the foxtrot. But Weitzenhoffer wasn't lost in nostalgia. He was more concerned about whether the university could meet their needs as well as it did when he was a freshman 60 years earlier.

"Giving someone an opportunity to find their dream in the theatre isn't easy," he said. "It's not like going into the business school or other places. It's the same with writing. You don't just sit in English class one day and suddenly decide, 'Oh, I'm going to be a writer.' It takes talent, it takes a lot of work and a lot of support to turn the theatre into a livelihood."

Something else far more important than the theatre to Max arose out of one of those many discussions at Wayne Alley's kitchen table. It's where he and Ayako Takahashi of Tokyo, Japan, decided to get married, which is how Max wound up being a father twice over. It was little like his own father, who married a much younger woman and had his first child in his 40s.

But it is Ayako who functions as the adult in the room, for she is the one who can get Max back on track when curiosity takes him on some sort

Home again

of tangent. Just as Fran's ability to charm anyone in her presence helped promote Max's Broadway career, Ayako has served as the pillar in the family Max never thought he would have. Her success as the full-time mother of their children Nikki and Owen, who are nearing college age, has guaranteed that they will not lack for college acceptance letters the way Max did. Both are fluent in Japanese, are well-traveled, mannerly and curious. Nikki is also gaining a national reputation in dressage. It seems she shares her love for horses with her mother, while Owen shares a passion for OU football with his father.

Ayako and Max met in a minivan, or touring bus, that was on its way from New York City to Philadelphia in the early spring of 1993, carrying those on board to the opening night of a play. What else could be more fitting? Ayako's college degree was in chemistry but her interest in the theatre and playwriting is what brought her to America. At the time Max was chairman of the Circle Repertory Company, whose mission was to establish an incubator where actors, directors, playwrights and designers could work together in the creation of experimental plays that might wind up on Broadway. For more than 30 years, Circle Rep. cultivated some of the most talented artists in the theatre.

The play they were going to see was called *Redwood Curtain* and starred Jeff Daniels. According to one review, "*Redwood Curtain* should go down as a textbook example of how the resident theatre circuit, which has proved so effective in fine-tuning the work of August Wilson before arriving on Broadway, can also go seriously awry—and how commercial theatre values can obscure the best intentions of theatre artists."

Weitzenhoffer was in a good mood as he carried on with Stewart Lane, a co-producer in *The Will Rogers Follies*, in the van. "I suspect we were acting like lunatics simply because we liked to have a good time," Max said.

Initially, he assumed Ayako probably thought he and Stewart must be gay, which he said is often the misperception regarding a man with an interest in the theatre and who wears colorful socks.

Mostly, he finds speculation about his sexuality amusing because it makes for some funny material, such as the time he almost got swept away by concert pianist Van Cliburn, who came to OU to play. "I didn't know him at all but he was strikingly good looking and had three little dogs that kept bounding around," Weitzenhoffer says "Anyway, we had dinner over at the Boyd House after the concert and I sat next to him. We discovered we knew a lot of the same people from New York and kept on chatting. Eventually, he said, 'I have to have a cigarette. Let's go to the terrace.' We went outside, and he says to me, 'You know, why don't you come down from time to time to Fort Worth and visit me. I'd like to have you down there.' That was a proposition. I went home and told my wife, 'you know, that's the first time I've been propositioned and actually thought about it.'"

On the other hand, the inquisitive stares two silly acting, smartly dressed middle-aged men were getting from the other passengers on the minivan on the way to Philadelphia that night did cast Max and Lane in an awkward light, as harmless as it may have been. Somewhere along the way, he began chatting with Ayako who had come to the states to pursue creative writing, and he found her quite interesting. She also happened to be very attractive and very young, 25 years younger than Max. "I liked her, and got her number," he said.

Their paths soon crossed again back in Oklahoma, this time intentionally, when he invited her to a black-tie fundraiser in Oklahoma City. Their relationship quickly expanded from that point into what he jokingly described as "the modern period," which he said almost encourages cohabitation. True to form, they moved in together, bought a lot across the creek from the Alleys, built a house, tore it down and then built a bigger house. The house was so personal to him that it looked like it belonged on a canvas.

Alley, who taught at the OU law school, and Max shared a lot of interests—the university, politics, art, and travel. More importantly, the Alleys embraced Ayako, no questions asked. "I know Max had been grieving for Fran, but I think Ayako had the kind of personality to be able to say, 'We are here to accept life as it is and that we have to look forward, not backward,'" Alley said. "I think Ayako was a lot of solace to him."

That eventually led to another knock on the Alleys' condominium door.

"You can marry people, right?" Max blurted out when Alley let him in. "How about marrying us?"

Normally rigid to a fault, Alley didn't quite make it to the kitchen table before answering, "How about Wednesday? How about coming to dinner?"

The ceremony lasted about a minute. Marie's brother was visiting from Germany, so he acted as a witness. He wasn't an American citizen, but he signed the form anyway.

A few years later along came two children, thrusting the big-time Broadway producer into a welcome, but awkward, role. He and Fran wanted to have children and had unsuccessfully tried to adopt a child. But that had been almost 30 years earlier.

"After the adoption fiasco Fran and I had, I never thought about having children," he said. "I had somehow convinced myself in my mind that because of my medical history—I blamed it on an advanced case of the mumps—that I was not capable of having a child. But Ayako, who was much younger, wanted to have a child, so I went and got tested."

When he returned home, Ayako asked him how he fared. His reply was accompanied by a certain amount of satisfaction: "The doctor said that if you don't have a child that it's not my fault."

The question now was whether Max's curiosity about new things would extend as far as learning how to change diapers.

This was at the height of the post-war, '50s era when the excitement of owning a passenger car with no windows created a magic that came with a European flair. It wasn't that the car was expensive; it was that you were just different from everybody else. And when you passed another convertible on the road, we blinked our lights at each other, creating the effect that you were tied to a whole group of people with the same idea.

Max's first car: the 1955 Corvette convertible, white with a red leather interior.

Collections

ext time. There always will be a next time, a time to get it right, a time to see the light. It doesn't matter if it's the first time or the 100th time, Max Weitzenhoffer approaches life the same way—with an air of confidence that masquerades as nonchalance and a fire in the belly obscured by the cummerband of the rich.

It took years, but best friend Gerald Gurney finally talked Max into taking a fly-fishing trip with him to Montana in the summer of 2017. They wouldn't exactly be roughing it—they would be staying in a swank fishing lodge with all the amenities, including a Swiss chef.

"This was Max's first time, so I told him not to overdo it, just bring the basics," Gurney said. "He came outfitted to the hilt. He must have spent two grand."

There was one thing for which Max could not prepare. The river was high which meant fishing was not good, not even for an experienced angler. Max did catch a small trout early on, but that was all for the next three days. "The point was that although he was unsuccessful, he was willing to keep trying," Gurney explained.

It's been a pattern throughout his life, whether it has been movies, autographs, guns, cars, art, the theatre, the university, his family or his home: Once Max bites into something, he won't let go until all reason has been exhausted. When it came to guns, for example, he wasn't content with purchasing a couple of rusty old revolvers used in a Dodge City gunfight. He bought so many rare firearms that when he donated his collection to the National Cowboy & Western Heritage Museum, it required a whole room to be built to properly display them.

But nothing has held his attention longer than his obsession with the automobile. It's not that he is an aficionado who collects a warehouse full of vintage cars and has a heart attack if a drop of oil from one of his baby's manifolds falls to the waxed floor. Max doesn't need to own a fleet. He just likes to admire the beauty of the automobile in general and own two or three of the really good ones.

"I think cars are probably the most beautiful thing I've ever seen, for some reason," he says. "I love the design of cars and I just love looking at them. They are just fantastic, and I can't tell you why. I know I just have to stop and look at them."

He also started driving about the time automakers began to truly design cars instead of merely assembling them. General Motors began to mold metal and fiberglass into shapes never seen before. He was alive for the introduction of air conditioning, wraparound windshields and all the other bells and whistles. The model that changed everything, of course, was the 1955 Corvette, which happened to be Weitzenhoffer's first car. It's hard to start at the top and work your way down, which is why he has furiously tried to maintain his high standards over time when it comes to the vehicles he owns.

His white 'Vette with an egg-crate grill and red interior was low and fast with a V8 engine. "I know I was fortunate to be able to get cars no one else would be able to get," he acknowledges. "But I did have a temporary melt-down when we went to pick that one up at the dealership."

When his father looked at it, the first thing out of his mouth to the sales-man who ordered it for them was, "It doesn't have white sidewalls. I wanted white sidewalls."

"You didn't order white sidewalls," the salesman answered.

"Then we are leaving," Max's father said.

Sure enough, they walked out and didn't return until there were white sidewalls on the car.

And so, a father's trait was passed on to the son: Don't ever settle. In addition to the Corvette with white sidewalls, he has owned two Mercedes, a Buick Riviera, three Cadillacs (two which were convertibles), four Aston Martins, two Rolls Royces, a Volkswagen Rabbit convertible, a Toyota Supra, five Jaguars, four Bentleys and a Ferrari.

He says his 1960 Mercedes 300SL Roadster tops his personal list of driv-ing machines, but when it comes to daydreaming about cars, he can't get the 1953 Cadillac Eldorado convertible out of his head. The first time he saw one he was at the Del Mar Racetrack; Harry James was driving it with actress Betty Grable next to him in the front seat.

Unfortunately, that's not the image his wife and children have of him behind the wheel. "We were having a discussion at dinner about who each of us was most like, and everyone came up with the same name for me: Toad of Toad Hall and his racing car. The one who is always running around the countryside in his sports car running over people," Max said, smiling.

If the car a man drives says all you need to know about him, then Weitzenhoffer could be described thusly: He knows what he likes and he's willing to pay for it. He also knows what he doesn't like, and dirty diapers are atop that list. That's true of anything he really values: cars, guns, art, the theatre. The home he and Ayako built in Norman after they got married and had children may be the best example of all. It reflects his taste and cautiously bears his soul as he is loathe to show it off, much the same way his mother kept her art collection to herself.

When he moved full-time to Norman with Ayako in 1995, Max purchased two empty lots less than a mile from the university and then built a 1930–40s-style house built for two on what had been a cow pasture.

He had been thinking about his dream house for a long time—one of the Rudolph Schindler variety. Schindler was an early 20th century Australian-American who designed as if there had never been houses before. But Weitzenhoffer wasn't ready to go all in yet, because what was happening on campus interested him more. This included the musical theatre and his growing involvement in the football program through Gurney, who at the time was the academic adviser for the athletic department.

Weitzenhoffer was approaching the age of 60. His father had lived to be only 65, yet Max did not feel the need to conduct a major inventory of his life. Broadway seemed a long way away, both figuratively and geographically, but he surprisingly didn't miss it. London, meanwhile, remained his favorite getaway when it came time to escape the summer heat in Oklahoma.

Life was slowing down. There were no more Broadway production meetings where the decision to close a show or not had millions of dollars in ramifications. About as heated as it got these days was a faculty meeting where the tensions might get high but where the stakes were always very low.

But a new century was at hand and there were hints that Max Weitzenhoffer wasn't going to be left behind after all. The first clue came in 1997 when he went to London with Burns to produce *Scissor Happy*, a comedy thriller, that closed after only three months. Five years had passed between *Eating Raoul* and *Scissor Happy*, the longest stretch of his career between shows. A year later, he and Burns produced *Defending the Caveman*, a one-man show that won a Laurence Olivier Award for Best Entertainment.

The part of the caveman is the one role Weitzenhoffer admits might have been perfect for him. "It was hysterically funny and mainly makes fun of men," he said. "It plays off the notion, mostly from the male perspective, that men are hunters and women are gatherers. I remember one of the examples is that a man is incapable of sitting in front of the TV without constantly changing channels because he's always hunting."

No, the role would not require much acting on Weitzenhoffer's part. *Caveman's* success also started a chain reaction that continues to this day, permanently reshaping his life.

First, his mother died in 2000, freeing up the trust fund she had managed and giving him the financial means to donate the $50 million art collection she had bequeathed him and build a $10 million family compound that has preserved his ties to Norman.

Secondly, he backed underdog Brad Henry, the winning candidate in the 2002 Oklahoma gubernatorial race which helped get Max a seat on the university's board of regents.

Finally, he took the biggest financial risk of his life at the age of 68 when he and Burns bought a group of second-tier, aging London theatres shortly before the financial crises of 2007 and 2008.

It's not that Weitzenhoffer had so much money that the exact amount was of no consequence. In the past, he had been forced to sell both valuable land and expensive cars to pay off creditors in the theatre. And he scrambled to pay for Fran's care when she was dying after his mother refused to help. Max's grandmother did leave him a lot of money, but his mother oversaw how the funds would be dispersed to Max as long as she lived. And charitable would not be a word that applied in this case. "My wife needed a lot of care toward the end, and when I called my mother asking for help, she told me the money was for a rainy day. This was much more than any ordinary rainy day. I called her friend David Wolpe, who was close to my wife, to get him to call my mother. He did help, telling her, "It's really pouring at Max's house. She sent me $10,000 a month. When Fran died, the checks immediately stopped."

When it came to his mother's art, she willed all of it to him but not with the understanding that he would pass it along to anyone else. University of Oklahoma President David Boren and his wife Molly had made several trips to La Jolla to encourage her to consider donating at least a few pieces of art to the university, but Max said she never expressed any sentimentality toward OU. Max made the one-of-its kind donation strictly to honor his father's love for the state of Oklahoma. "Surprisingly, about the only thing she would have done is turn the house on Drury Lane into a public museum, but Nichols Hills' ordinances wouldn't have allowed for that," Max said.

Gaining access to his trust fund triggered several important events. For the first time in his life, it freed him from his mother's grip. It also minimized his risk in 2001 when he purchased the Vaudeville Theatre in London, and, finally, it allowed him to think way out of the box when he and Ayako started having children and needed more room. "We had added a pool, a pool house and a conservatory and there was no way to make the first house any bigger," he said.

There were five vacant lots in the same cul-de-sac where they had built their deco-style, two-bedroom home in '95, so Max bought all five and hired prominent modernist architect Hugh Jacobson of Washington, D.C., to design and oversee construction. What Max wanted was what Jacobson had few equals in delivering: a house with space, lots of glass and accented by water and trees.

"What you have to remember is the concept of all the houses of Schindler-style that I liked were based originally on Japanese designs with sliding doors and panels. They're very simple-minded, architecturally," Weitzenhoffer said.

What Weitzenhoffer got was a piece of one-of-a-kind art, a breathtaking sculpture that happened to come with bedrooms and a kitchen, and that blended concrete, marble, water, light and open space like Kandinsky did colors. It was an abstract at which to marvel, provided the eye is allowed to wander around long enough to appreciate the mood that has been created.

"During construction I was standing in the yard outside the conservatory thinking how my father told me you shouldn't look on your home as an investment," Max recalled. "Knowing him as well as I did and given the enormous cost of this house, I was immediately waiting to be struck by a lightning bolt."

It's a glass house but it is not necessarily a show piece, because much of its innate beauty is hidden from the street. Except for a large porthole over the front door, there are no windows across the front of the house. The earth-toned concrete façade seems content to let a line of Japanese non-bearing cherry trees serve as a welcoming party. The 12,000 square foot main house is the centerpiece of what amounts to a compound, which also features a 2,100 square-foot guest house across the street, a conservatory and a wraparound pool with a disappearing edge that surrounds almost half of the back and one side of the house. It also includes steep-pitched green metal roofs on both houses that some of the neighbors had a fit about in the beginning. Those with a more traditional taste would probably say that the $10 million Weitzenhoffer spent could have bought a lot of crown molding, archways and stately columns instead of being spent in search of minimalism. But then they haven't seen the huge commercial heating and cooling system behind the guest house. Earl Cooper, the manager of the Weitzenhoffer's estate, says its pipes cross under the street to the main house and keeps it as humidity-free as any museum so that Max can hang his art anywhere he chooses.

Some of the architectural touches that bring Weitzenhoffer pleasure: A sprawling atrium that is the visual centerpiece of the house. Sun filters through the skylights overhead and through a row of beams that overhang a reflection pool that runs almost the entire length of the ground floor. If you stand at the back edge of the pool and face the front, the reflection off the water forms an imaginary stairway that appears to lead right into the water. Four huge recessed planters containing Kentia palms ring either side of the pool, creating a lush tropical effect.

All the glass in the house—and glass is on three sides of the ground floor—is floor-to-ceiling and there is no molding where the glass meets the floor. Also, there is no molding between the panes of glass that intersect wherever there is a right angle. Instead, the glass joins itself. Because each panel weighs about 1,200 pounds, a crane had to lift each one over the entire house before it could be installed.

The absence of molding provides a seamless line of sight from the living room to the patio which serves as a bridge between the main floor and the outdoor pool, and then across to the dining room, which is on the other side of the patio.

"I always see water when I sit in the back part of the house, and that's the feeling I wanted, along with seeing something green, which is why we planted a massive amount of bamboo behind the pool," Max said. "It stays green all year."

The house has high ceilings throughout. There is a lot of recessed directional lighting but the forced air that heats and cools the house isn't delivered through vents or ducts. It flows from long, narrow slats in the ceilings of each room. For privacy, push-button operated ceiling-to-floor shades pop out from above.

The sliding doors have stainless steel levers instead of handles or knobs, which is in line with the minimalist style Max sought. "I wanted a house that looked like the houses in California in the 1930s," he said.

Ayako calls the house an Egyptian pyramid, which makes him the King Tut of Norman. In some ways, gaining passage into Weitzenhoffer's private world is as difficult as locating the secret burial chambers of the pharaohs. "I'm not being negative about it, but even the few people that come in here hardly ever say anything about my taste. Most don't say anything, but I think they must be thinking, 'What the shit is this?'"

In effect, he's been in the opinion business his whole career, whether it was as an art dealer or a producer. Did the critics like it? Did the audience think it was to die for? The kind of house he chose to build is not up for that kind of debate. It was strictly personal.

"I had been waiting more than 40 years for something like this, ever since I really started thinking about architecture and livable space," he said. "This has been the culmination of a long mental process."

Along the way Max gravitated to the offerings of modernist architect Richard Neutra, who migrated from Austria to California where he was influenced by Schindler and Frank Lloyd Wright. Benefiting from the development of new materials and manufacturing techniques, Neutra felt emboldened to expand the creative process. His use of glass spaces in what the book *Furniture & Interiors of the 1940s* referred to as the continual battle for the fight for freedom were showcased in the Kaufman House in the hills near Palm Springs, California. Instead of hills, Weitzenhoffer chose to be surrounded by water and greenery. The dining room in the Kaufman House, for example, opened onto the patio, where a perforated interior wall could be positioned to separate a covered outdoor living room with a fireplace. Glass was utilized with virtually no support, reinforcing the communication between inside and outside spaces.

Increased housing demand, optimism that welled up in a post-war world and new products that were emerging from research laboratories also allowed architects and designers to rethink furniture. Long before he was constructing his new home in Norman, Weitzenhoffer hardly spent a day in New York City where he didn't have contact with exclusive furniture dealers who specialized in the moderns. He looked at furniture as art, and he was always looking to make contact with a piece that spoke back to him.

Collections

The dining room table in Ayako and Max's home features chairs that were once in composer George Gershwin's New York apartment.

Much of what he has acquired somewhere along the line now holds places of prominence in his home. The dining room table is Dutch, but the chairs were designed by George Gershwin and came from Gershwin's apartment in New York. The sofa and two chairs in the living room were among the set decorations that had been left behind from a Noel Coward show and were going to be discarded. There's a circa 1937 Alvar Aalto armchair in the foyer that attests to Aalto's humanism and realism. Weitzenhoffer also began acquiring pieces by James Mont, called the "Bad Boy of American Design," including a desk and all the furniture in the breakfast room, long before others discovered him. Mont had been convicted of assault when he attacked a lampshade designer in his apartment, but those looking for a counter-balance to restrained modernism found it in his bold and exotic pieces, along with forgiveness. Max has taken sculptures from the 1930s that interest him and converted them into table lamps, crowning them with hand-painted lampshades he had commissioned. The throw rugs in front of the fireplace are 1930s Art Deco.

In two concessions to Max, the original architect gave him an ample amount of built-in box shelves to store his printed treasures and eliminated the architectural plan to put a television in the master bedroom that popped out of a table when it was turned on. "My attitude is that electronic equipment has its own design and you therefore want to see it," Max said. "And there's no point in hiding everything."

Max fired his architect because he was tired of waiting for things to get done. "We were getting behind, and it was costing a fortune," he said. "Hugh now maintains it's not his house, but I don't care."

That's because, by any measure, it is a Weitzenhoffer house, and there always seems to be a little intrigue associated with that name.

The Norman house. This house embodies everything that is in my head and I find it stimulating on a personal level, but I don't expect it to mean anything to others because it's the personal things that reside here that make it what it is. They represent a lot of stories that matter to me, whether they are objects of art, books, or architectural lines.

All your doors are open

By the end of 2002 Max Weitzenhoffer had a wife, a new house and two children. The music theatre program he had created at the University of Oklahoma was attracting top-notch talent from around the country. He had recently purchased a playhouse in London where he liked to hang out, and he was producing again with a new partner who saw things the way he did. On top of that, life was so good that he could afford to donate more than $50 million in artwork to his alma mater. At the age of 63, he had pretty much covered all the bases.

Well, almost.

Earlier that year his high school classmate Fred Gipson, the general counsel for the University of Oklahoma, told him there was someone he wanted Max to meet. Weitzenhoffer really didn't have much of a clue as to who Brad Henry was, other than he knew Henry was a long-shot Democrat running for governor in a state that was rapidly trending Republican. Max almost always voted Republican, which was one reason he hadn't paid much attention to Henry. The other was that Henry was a state senator from another district (Shawnee, Oklahoma) who didn't seem to have an interest in being the loudest voice in the room.

They met over lunch and weren't long into their discussion when Weitzenhoffer concluded that he liked the man. He thought Henry was reasonable and authentic. Even better, Henry wasn't Steve Largent, a former National Football League Hall of Fame player and a Republican U.S. Congressman from Tulsa, who was a heavy favorite to win the race. For his part, Max thought Largent attached himself too much to God. "God isn't running everybody's lives," Max explained.

Henry got the maximum allowable campaign contribution from Weitzenhoffer, and then Max gave him something even more valuable than money. Weitzenhoffer introduced him to Larry Wade, Max's best friend who was the publisher of the *Elk City Daily News*, a prominent voice in western Oklahoma. Wade liked Henry, too, and wrote an editorial endorsing him, which caused a lot of other newspapers and Oklahomans in general to re-examine Henry's chances of winning.

In the 2002 general election, Henry defeated Largent by 7,000 votes, the third-smallest vote differential in state history. As soon as Henry took office, Gipson relayed a message from new governor that he wanted to appoint Weitzenhoffer to the seven-member University of Oklahoma Board of Regents.

Max was seriously tempted but his first thought was that the appointment should go to Wade, whose endorsement was a big boon to Henry's

Max and his best friend and fellow OU regent Larry Wade.

election chances. "I said, yes, but what about Larry? Fred said Larry would get the next one."

There was one final moment of hesitancy when Weitzenhoffer realized the university's conflict-of-interest rules would prevent him from serving simultaneously on both the board of regents and as director of the musical theatre program. "I wasn't sure I wanted to give that up," he said. "Ultimately, I realized that I could really add something positive to the university as a whole and contribute a perspective as a faculty member that might be beneficial to the board."

What clinched the deal was his knowledge that President Boren was pushing Henry to appoint his own candidate. "Brad really didn't want to do that, so I said, 'Well, I'll do it,'" Max acknowledged. "What made it a bigger responsibility was that I was replacing Mary Jane Noble, who was legendary."

Given that Weitzenhoffer had just bestowed the largest gift of its kind in the history of higher education, Henry knew that it would be difficult for Boren, who was riding a wave of popularity at the time (OU had won a national football championship a year earlier) to complain.

Weitzenhoffer went on to serve 14 years on the board, including two stints as chairman, and became embroiled in several major controversies along the way. All the while he was a minor thorn in Boren's side because Max told him what he thought, not what he assumed Boren wanted to hear. From his point of view, Weitzenhoffer doesn't believe he had much influence on Boren, whose intellect, personality and political skills enabled him to keep a firm grip on almost every aspect of the university from the board on down. Sometimes it felt like the Boren locomotive was rolling unabated down the tracks and there weren't any crossing gates to protect anything

All your doors are open

that got in the way. Weitzenhoffer blames himself for some of that with this caveat: "You have to remember that to get anything done as a regent, you need three other votes."

When it came to his service on the board, Weitzenhoffer's two most personally rewarding accomplishments came from working with the presidents of Rogers State and Cameron State as chairman of the committees that oversaw those two schools and promoting the importance of scholar athletes to the university.

His meetings with Rogers State president Joe Wiley occasionally took place at the casino near Claremore over a few drinks and some blackjack. One brainstorm that grew out of it was Weitzenhoffer's suggestion that Rogers should offer a program in gaming design, as only one other college in the country had a similar program at the time. In order to facilitate the rapid growth of the casino gaming industry, he had suggested the same idea to Boren, who wasn't interested. "We both realized that to be successful Rogers would have to offer programs that nobody else did," Weitzenhoffer said. "The amazing thing is Joe got it approved by the Legislature, which nobody thought he would."

Because he lived in Norman, the pull of gravity from the highly successful OU athletic program was something Max could not escape, not that he was looking to hide. As a regent, he traveled with the football team to all its road games and was joined by his son Owen as soon as he was old enough to roam the sidelines with his father. He compares those times to the memories his father made for him when they took the train to Sooner road games in the Bud Wilkinson era. Because he was around the athletic department so much, Max heard about the football program's wants and needs from key members of the department and then shared that information with other members of the board of regents. Fewer programs were more important to the regents than the football program. Impressed by the quality of student athletes the university was attracting, Max started donating $10,000 annually to sponsor the Scholar Athlete Breakfast. He also was the one who came up with the idea of "endowing" positions on the OU football team after reading about a similar program at Penn State University. Ultimately, Weitzenhoffer contributed $250,000 to have the quarterback position named after him. Later, he had it switched to his son Owen's name. The jersey the athletic department presented him with, which features "Weitzenhoffer" and the numeral "1" on the back, is one of his most cherished possessions because it will forever link his family to the football program and is a continuation of a tradition inspired by his father. To Max, that jersey means more to him than any building that could be named after him.

It would be hard to overstate the impact of Sooner football on the state of Oklahoma. The word "Sooner" was first used after the Land Run of 1889 to describe settlers who entered the Unassigned Lands before the

All your doors are open

Max with Heisman Trophy winner Sam Bradford along with OU Vice President and athletic director Joe Castiglione (left) and head football coach Bob Stoops (right).

Bud Wilkerson. University of Oklahoma Athletics Department

Barry Switzer. University of Oklahoma Athletics Department

Bob Stoops. University of Oklahoma Athletics Department

designated starting time. The term derived from a section in the Indian Appropriation Act of March 2, 1889, which became known as the "sooner clause." According to the Oklahoma Historical Society, it stated that no person should be permitted to enter upon and occupy the land before the time designated in the president's opening proclamation and that anyone who violated the provision would be denied a right to own land.

In the estimation of those who played by the rules, the Sooners were lower than the dirt they came to claim until 1908 when the University of Oklahoma adopted the name "Sooners" for its football team. Ten years later, Oklahomans considered the term to be a testament to their pride and progressivism, and Oklahoma has since been known as the Sooner State, although it has never been thus designated by statute or resolution.

The marketing genius who sold the state on making it believe that Sooners were actually the "good guys" could not have foreseen exactly how good the Sooners would become. In the postwar era of college football (1946–2017), the University of Oklahoma ranks first in the number of victories (640), first in the number of consensus All-American players, tied for first with Alabama for the most number of NCAA-recognized national titles and first with the longest winning streak of 47 games. And Oklahoma has produced six Heisman Trophy winners, an award which recognizes the best player in college football.

Weitzenhoffer's time on the board of regents overlapped the Coach Bob Stoops era, another golden age of Oklahoma football in the same vein as the eras of coaches Bud Wilkinson and Barry Switzer. But for all the great times Max witnessed at the sold-out Gaylord Family Memorial Stadium there is one moment, played out secretly away from the roar of the crowd, that he thinks will haunt the university for a long time.

As Weitzenhoffer sat in a luncheon meeting with other members of the University of Oklahoma Board of Regents in Tulsa, Oklahoma, on Sept. 12, 2011, it appeared they were on the verge of making history. A majority of the regents had agreed the university would accept an invitation to join the newly expanded Pacific 12 Conference, which reportedly was all but a formality, ending a two-year roller-coaster ride involving OU's future athletic conference affiliation. Now, there was only one more hurdle to go—university president David Boren, who seemed bent on holding the Big 12 Conference together. At the very least, he appeared opposed to leaving the conference for greener pastures unless fellow member Oklahoma State University went with them. In addition, the way Weitzenhoffer understood it, the Pac-12 only wanted the Sooners at that point.

"We told David that the Pac-12 would still make us an offer to join their conference, and that we, as regents, had decided we would accept it without OSU, period," Weitzenhoffer said. "We told him it was an order from the board and that he was not to say anything about it until it was official."

Previously, nothing had gone as planned for the Sooners when it came to conference alignment. A year earlier, board members thought there was a deal in place for several Big 12 schools—Oklahoma, Oklahoma State and the University of Texas—to move to what was then the Pac 10, but Weitzenhoffer said that at the last minute Texas refused to give up its financially lucrative Longhorn Television Network, which was to be a condition of acceptance. The move by Texas to create its own television partnership with ESPN so angered other members of the Big 12 Conference that it was cited as one of the main reasons Nebraska University had pulled out of the Big 12 and joined the Big 10 Conference, and why Texas A&M University and the University of Missouri left the Big 12 for the Southeastern Conference. The University of Colorado, another Big 12 member, then jumped to the Pac 10, joining Utah, which made it a 12-team league.

Weitzenhoffer said it wasn't the precarious situation the Big 12 had found itself in after losing four of its established members that was driving their decision. They simply thought by aligning with some of the finest academic institutions in the country—Stanford, Cal-Berkeley, UCLA and the University of Southern California—the reputation of the University of Oklahoma would be forever enhanced. "Those schools are head-and-shoulders better academically than all of the schools in the Big 12 besides Texas," Weitzenhoffer stressed.

Weitzenhoffer said he had been holding informal conversations for more than a year with the vice-chair of the Pac-12 to prepare for this day. "It

David Boren. Courtesy of the University of Oklahoma Foundation

would have been great for our law school to be associated with Stanford and it would have been great for our fine arts programs to be able to do exchanges with UCLA and USC," Weitzenhoffer said. "And the West Coast would have been good for our research and fundraising efforts. This was about much more than athletics."

Boren took the news without objection, Weitzenhoffer said, but at one point during lunch he excused himself to take a telephone call and didn't return for more than half an hour. Before holding his usual post-board meeting press conference that afternoon, Boren was instructed by the regents to not divulge anything regarding a potential invitation from the Pac-12, Weitzenhoffer said.

But Boren apparently had his own ideas because at the press conference he shocked the board by claiming the rumor that Oklahoma would join the Pac-12 was not true and that the university had been merely negotiating with the Pac-12 in hopes of enhancing its position with the Big 12 Conference.

Within minutes, Weitzenhoffer said OU's legal counsel, which had been involved in the discussions with the Pac-12, got a telephone call from their colleagues in the Pac-12 asking them why Boren threw them under the bus. "I got an email a few minutes later saying, 'Look what you did to us

All your doors are open

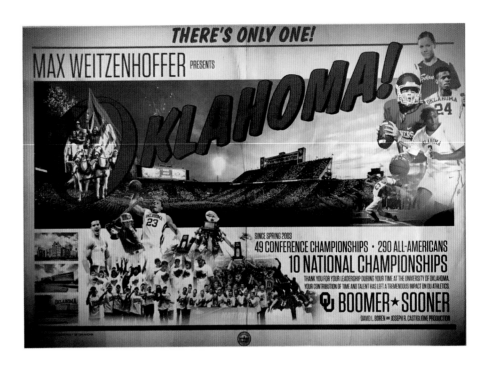

". . . We don't want to ever see you again. We hope you find someplace else," Weitzenhoffer said.

Weitzenhoffer said he doesn't know who Boren was on the telephone with that day and he doesn't know what drove Boren to basically end negotiations with the Pac-12. The regents had considered the possibility that the Oklahoma Legislature, particularly the Oklahoma State graduates among them, would retaliate against OU if it went anywhere without taking OSU. "We knew that there would be a backlash, but we also knew we could weather the financial hit and that would be forgotten within a few years," Weitzenhoffer said.

There was also talk that some OU coaches were opposed to the move because of the travel and recruiting implications that could affect both players and fans. While OU alumni in California would relish being able to regularly see the Sooners in person, those from Oklahoma and Texas would be forced to travel greater distances for many of the road games.

As a selling point, Weitzenhoffer referenced the time he traveled with the Sooners for a game at Cal-Berkeley where he saw parking spaces reserved for Nobel Laureates at the football stadium. That was the future he foresaw for Oklahoma if it switched conferences.

On the way back to Oklahoma City after Boren's press conference, Weitzenhoffer said he and the other regents felt hopeless. "We kept thinking, who was he talking to on the phone? He had put us in a position where we lost the deal, so there was nothing more we could do about it."

The board may have been justified in firing Boren, but Weitzenhoffer said that wasn't an option because he was a skilled fundraiser who was highly regarded by an important segment of the donor base. Boren also had a long

All your doors are open

198

list of accomplishments to his credit, starting with the fact that he hired athletic director Joe Castiglione, who hired Stoops, who in turn helped restore the grandeur of OU football after it cratered in the early 1990s with Switzer's departure as coach. In the beginning, Oklahoma measured success by the size of its wheat crop. Then oil production became the gauge for prosperity. Ultimately, it was OU's football record that people cared about most.

More than anything, Boren's ability to circumvent the wishes of his board when it came to determining what was in the best long-term interest for OU further demonstrated the hold he had over the university for more than two decades. Weitzenhoffer was alternately amazed and frustrated by Boren's forceful management style which was driven by his political instincts, an ultra-conservative philosophy when it came to grooming students for adulthood and a reluctance to fully embrace a collegial atmosphere that usually accompanies such a setting.

Prone to flippancy at inopportune times and noted for saying what he thought, Weitzenhoffer could prove to be a real challenge for a man such as Boren. "David is a brilliant man but there are occasions when you can see right through him," Weitzenhoffer said. "David was a very good governor and United States senator. But he wanted to be president of the United States. And he has no sense of humor about it, because when he moved in as president over there in the big office he has, I said to him one day, 'Well, you wanted an oval office, and here it is.' But that didn't go over very well."

The one word Weitzenhoffer would use to describe Boren, who retired in 2018 after 24 years as president, is "effective," which leaves beauty in the eye of the beholder. The word was carefully chosen because there were times "when effectiveness can be a negative from my point of view."

Specifically, Weitzenhoffer thinks Boren surrounded himself with too many vice-presidents and fired, hired and then fired too many deans while not putting enough women in positions of authority. Weitzenhoffer also believed Boren placed too much emphasis on his National Merit Scholars Program, which covered most costs for high school students who scored in the top one percent on a standardized test, and not enough on tending to the needs of regular students.

For example, Weitzenhoffer found Boren's policies regarding student conduct to be too restrictive while punishment was overly harsh. Football game days were a metaphor for how the campus functioned in general. Every college campus has its own personality, but those that take football seriously usually share one characteristic—game days are fun for one and all. Granted, fun can get out of hand, but Weitzenhoffer thought it was a mistake for Boren to no longer allow fraternities and sororities to have open houses on football game days where parents could drop in for a visit. "When Larry Wade and I were here, my dad and Larry's father would come over, have a

All your doors are open

drink maybe and chat with each other," Max said. "The whole atmosphere was more like what I see at all the other universities I saw on game day when I was traveling with the team. Then, there's the tailgate parties. We have them, but it appears that we want to keep them out of sight."

It's not that Weitzenhoffer is advocating for OU to aspire to make the annual top ten list of party schools. And he recognizes that his views on, say, alcohol, may be too extreme for many Oklahomans. But it is more of a cumulative thing than one specific thing, Weitzenhoffer emphasized, saying "I don't think a great university can function without units that have degrees of autonomy."

Over time, Weitzenhoffer believed Boren's decisions were driven more by what was best for the university's image instead of carrying out the university's responsibility to prepare students for the real world. "He even had his own press agent in addition to the university's information office," Weitzenhoffer said. "What college president needs his own press agent? I've worked with some of the best people in the world in my career, and I've never seen anyone like David Boren."

For example, Weitzenhoffer said Boren gravitated to his intellectual equals, i.e. his Merit Scholarship program and the Crimson Club, at all costs. "I know he had no use for fraternities and sororities, but what he didn't realize is that most of the big donors, like myself, were all C students. I've maintained the people who really give are the batch of regular students here that are getting degrees but spend a little more time having a good time than they should. But then they get jobs and make a lot of money."

While Weitzenhoffer credits Boren for totally supporting his efforts to establish the musical theatre program and giving his mother's art collection a place of prominence at the university, he thinks that in the end Boren probably considered him to be more trouble than he was worth, particularly when Max literally lived down the street from campus and was "always around." In addition, he was the only regent in the history of the board of regents who had ever been a faculty member before joining the board, which made him well acquainted with the faculty's perspective and gave him insight into the administrative side of the university. "The point was when it came to regents' meetings or committee meetings, yes, the president and I got crosswise a lot of times because I looked at things completely differently. I looked at things more in the context of the history of the university, how we arrived at this point in time versus the need to change and whether the student body would be all the better for it."

No doubt, Boren had a highly successful run as president. He expanded enrollment, managed to hold down tuition increases despite a big reduction in the amount of funding appropriated by the state legislature, greatly improved campus infrastructure and raised the national stature of the university. "For all of my concerns, I must point out that the President

Boren immensely improved the academic standards and reputation of the university," Weitzenhoffer said. "And because he had a great career as governor of Oklahoma and as a U.S. Senator, he was able to transform the university through not only his intellect but with his ability to attract a never-ending stream of world leaders and cultural icons to campus, from Mikhail Gorbachev to Margaret Thatcher."

Given that eight years is the average length of tenure for a college president, Boren simply stayed too long, in Weitzenhoffer's view. "After 20 years on the job, I don't think there was any area of the university he didn't think he was an expert in. But then I know he cared a great deal about the university, too."

His assessment of Boren's tenure obviously was adversely influenced by the two incidents in which Weitzenhoffer became embroiled, the first of which left a permanent scar. "It's the most hurtful thing I've done in my whole life and I did it myself because I never realized the depth of what can exist in small town America," he said.

It began innocently enough when President Boren asked Weitzenhoffer, who was then a member of the board of regents, to see what he could

All your doors are open

201

do to get the band moving with more precision and determination. Both thought the OU marching band was boring, not up to par with the signature bands at Ohio State or Notre Dame, and that it was time to go outside the university to find a replacement for the band director. Weitzenhoffer identified a candidate from the University of Wisconsin he considered to be the solution. It wasn't long before people were trying to run the new director out of town as well as malign Weitzenhoffer, who was later sued by the one-time hand-picked candidate to succeed the retiring band director, claiming she didn't get the job because she was a woman.

The controversy played out in a public manner that pitted current and former band members against the new band director and the administration, tainted by allegations that Weitzenhoffer had some sort of relationship with the person he recommended. "One day my friend Gerald Gurney told me not to go home because TV trucks were in front of my house," Max recalls. "I was accused of 'knowing him' in Wisconsin. I don't mind being called homosexual. God may not love them, but I could care less. My answer was, 'He's not my type.' But the fact of the matter is what they did to him was a disgrace," Weitzenhoffer said. "You don't destroy someone over the fact that he wanted to make changes in the band."

He thinks the controversy over the resignation of the band director might have gone differently if Boren had supported the band director more vociferously from the beginning, just as he remains convinced Boren's decision to agree to joint ownership of his mother's 1886 painting "Shepherdess Bringing in Sheep" by Camille Pissarro had more to do with Boren's desire to gain financial support for a statewide ballot initiative to increase funding for higher education than it did with the principle of the matter or the public relations problem the Pissarro was creating for the university.

Weitzenhoffer made a gift of the Pissarro and more than 25 other major works of art to the University of Oklahoma Foundation not long after his mother's death. One of her favorites was the "Shepherdess," which she purchased from David Findlay's gallery in 1957. Prior to World War II, it had been owned first by Theophile Bader, who co-founded the department chain Galeries Lafayette and later by his daughter Yvonne and her husband Raoul Meyer. After Germany invaded France, the painting was seized by the Nazis from a vault where it had been stored for safekeeping.

The painting eventually wound up in Switzerland, which is when its ownership came in question. One version is that the man who purchased it had a questionable reputation for handling stolen art. He offered to sell it back to Yvonne and Raoul Meyer, but they refused, claiming they already owned it, and the couple sued to get the painting back. However, a Swiss court ruled against them, saying the Meyers could not prove that its current owner knew the painting had been stolen. The painting changed ownership several times before Clara Weitzenhoffer bought it, and nothing more was said about it until around 2009 when an associate curator at the Indianapolis Museum of Art questioned the chain of custody. Three years later, Leone Meyer, who was adopted by Yvonne and Raul Meyer in 1946 and whose own family died in the Holocaust at Auschwitz, set out to reclaim the painting by filing a lawsuit in New York. The university and the OU Foundation initially challenged her, arguing that Meyer had not been diligent in pursuing her claim and that she had avoided filing suit in Oklahoma to avoid the state's more restrictive statute of limitations.

Although the University won the initial round in court forcing Meyer to refile her lawsuit in Oklahoma, public sentiment quickly shifted to her side as Boren began to feel the heat from the Jewish community as well as from students, faculty members and some lawmakers. While it's likely that the university could have prevailed in state court based on previous legal rulings, Boren quickly agreed to a settlement by which Meyer got custody of the painting while the university was allowed to continue to display it on a rotating basis.

Weitzenhoffer, who was not a party to the lawsuit and was not involved in settlement negotiations, remained mostly silent in the face of accusations that his mother knowingly had purchased stolen art. "What I will say is that if I had still owned the painting and this had happened, I would not have settled," he said. "Now, if the original owner had perished in a concentration camp and I had been approached by the family, that would have been different. I would have had no compunction about returning it."

Weitzenhoffer doesn't believe that is the case in this instance. "The original owner did not spend the war in duress," he emphasized. "I think he tried to get the painting back a number of times, and when it was offered back to him, he didn't want it. Also, the painting was never hidden. It was in public view for a number of years. In the end, I believe it was given to somebody who did not have a relationship to the painting."

Then again, life is not fair. Often, it wears us down toward the end. When Weitzenhoffer was honored at the completion of his final term on the board of regents, he harkened back to his days as a student at OU and profusely thanked the professors for their efforts on his behalf. While he was grateful, there was some doubt whether he was still capable of being propelled from his seat in uncontainable joy on opening night at the theatre.

"I was talking to my wife, complaining about when I got off the board of regents . . . I was moaning and groaning and complaining, and she said, 'Why don't you realize that for most people your age, all the doors are closed. All your doors are open.'"

It made him think of London. The question was would it make him think of Broadway, as well.

Nimax Theatres/London. The West End is the mirror image of what Broadway was in its Golden Age, although it is changing, too. But the formation and growth of Nimax with Nica Burns has been a huge second act in the theatre for me. There's nothing wrong with standing outside the Palace Theatre and looking up and seeing that *Harry Potter* is playing inside. It's about as exciting a feeling as one can have.

"MALKOVICH & STEVENSON...
ACTING TO DIE FOR" CITY LIMITS
"A STUDY OF SEXUAL PASSION"
GUARDIAN
"HYPNOTIC" "BREATHTAKING"
DAILY MAIL WHAT'S ON
"DANGEROUSLY ELECTRIFYING"
OBSERVER
"THE MOST EXCITING ACTOR SINCE BRANDO"
GUARDIAN

ROBERT FOX LIMITED, JAMES B. FREYDBERG, ROBERT G. PERKINS AND MAX WEITZENHOFFER
BY ARRANGEMENT WITH STOLL MOSS THEATRES LTD
PRESENT THE HAMPSTEAD THEATRE PRODUCTION OF

JOHN MALKOVICH   JULIET STEVENSON
MICHAEL SIMKINS   LOU LIBERATORE

IN
BURN THIS
BY
LANFORD WILSON

DIRECTED BY
ROBERT ALLAN ACKERMAN

SET DESIGNED BY   COSTUMES DESIGNED BY   LIGHTING DESIGNED BY   ORIGINAL MUSIC BY
EILEEN DISS   TOM RAND   MICK HUGHES   PETER KATER

ORIGINALLY PRODUCED BY CIRCLE REPERTORY COMPANY, TANYA BERESIN, ARTISTIC DIRECTOR AND MARK TAPER FORUM, GORDON DAVIDSON, ARTISTIC DIRECTOR.
ORIGINALLY PRODUCED ON BROADWAY BY JAMES B. FREYDBERG, STEPHEN GRAHAM, SUSAN QUINT GALLIN, MAX WEITZENHOFFER

LIMITED SEASON TO 29 SEPTEMBER
LYRIC THEATRE
SHAFTESBURY AVENUE, LONDON W1 A STOLL MOSS THEATRE

The Show goes on

"I am a showman by profession . . .And all the gilding shall make nothing else of me."
—— P.T. BARNUM

One of the things that made the circus so enticing was a primeval sense that something could go wrong at any moment, that the audience was teetering on the edge along with the performers. That was back when trapeze artists didn't work with nets underneath them, when they flew through the air and hoped for the best. And the lions looked menacing enough that there was a sense they could maul the lion tamer whenever they got the notion, and that cracking a whip would be a waste of energy. It was hard to know where the manufactured suspense ended and when genuine fear was born.

But there was only one P.T. Barnum, so Max Weitzenhoffer settled for trying to duplicate that brand of emotion on stage minus the blood, broken bones and animal torture.

"For the theatre to work, you really have to take your audience and move them out of the mental state they were in when they walked in and take them to another world," Max has often said.

The play *Dracula* opens with Lucy turning on the radio. Jeanette MacDonald is singing a song called *Dream Lover*, a clever literary device that foretells how Dracula will come to her in the second act with seduction on his mind. Such emotion is easier to evoke when the theme is of star-crossed lovers in a straight play. But it can work in musicals, too, which is why the *Phantom of the Opera* was so successful where, by the last scene, the audience was desperately trying to save the Phantom from his fate. Sometimes the emotion is derived from the staging, such as in *Les Misérables* where Fantine died alone on stage, a moving performance that is made more emotional because of the way the lighting was engineered. Or it can work with a song, such as Ray Bolger singing *Once Upon a Time* in the 1962 musical *The All-American*.

But the charm of the theatre isn't that which is peeled off the pages of a script and brought to life by a gifted performer. What sets it apart from the movies or television is that everyone inside the theatre is breathing the same air at the same time and, if it goes right, they are all crying, laughing or holding their collective breaths together.

"When the curtain goes up, there isn't any room for mistakes," Weitzenhoffer said, which is why the man who keeps pursuing the "What's next?"

in life with his eye on the "It" factor is drawn to the stage, despite his unquenching thirst for a good movie.

There are no outtakes in the theatre. There is only the exit sign if you don't like what's taking place on stage. The cast members must be in rhythm from beginning to end, and the audience doesn't want to see them botching their lines. Furthermore, the audience will get very uncomfortable if it catches on that the actors are uncomfortable, at which point everybody is uncomfortable. And it's not ever a possibility that the director will come on stage and say, "I'm sorry, we've done an hour of this play, but now we have to go back and start all over again because something happened in Act One that we hadn't anticipated."

Max Weitzenhoffer adores the movies and movie actors (he has collected their autographs and other memorabilia in droves over the years), but he fully realizes that they are there as part of a package that is basically controlled by the director. "They don't have to sit down and learn three hours of something they have to do eight times a week," he says. "In Hollywood they get some pages of dialogue that tells them what they are going to shoot that day. And it may have nothing to do with what they did the day before. I'm not saying it's easy, but it is vastly different from the stage, which is why a lot of actors don't do Broadway."

This also is why few producers make a career of Broadway, much less profit from it. Max lasted longer than most, but eventually the odds caught up with him, too. He blamed it on the diminishing pool of extraordinary full-time playwrights, a growing obsession with political correctness, enormous production costs, spiraling ticket prices and the number of corporate sponsors it took to feed the beast. But every one of those reasons missed the mark. For as much as Broadway had changed in his estimation, the truth was it was Weitzenhoffer who had inexplicitly rejected the ever-changing nature of the theatre in what could be best described as a misguided attempt to prevent a comfortable but decidedly worn favorite old easy chair from being cast to the curb as part of his wife's redecorating project.

At the age of 79, Max was starting to see the change as something for which he never seemed to have time for – growing old. For one thing, his days as a major force on the University of Oklahoma Board of Regents and the challenges that came with the position had come to an end. For another, his two children would soon be ready for college and careers of their own. His own mortality and place in the world were coming into question in his mind and no amount of success in the theatre business could seem to change his perspective, even if London was his favorite city in the world. "Do I really care if my name is on top of our theatres in the West End when I'm not here any longer, unless, of course, I get to stay as a ghost?" he said in a moment of reflection. "There will come a time when I am just a footnote."

Sadly, when it came to taking on new challenges on the stage, it appeared that about the only hill that Max had any interest in climbing was one of the sandstone buttes that ring Monument Valley on the Arizona-Utah border in what is called the Four Corners. Weitzenhoffer has seen it on screen hundreds of times but he has never seen Monument Valley in person. Maybe there he could use his imagination to find Lt. Colonel Owen Thursday (Henry Fonda) and Capt. Kirby York (John Wayne) riding horseback across the parched desert to tame the fictional West created by director John Ford, with or without the cooperation of the aggrieved original inhabitants of a sparse land. To Max it was so simple. The setting was majestic with a line of cavalry men followed by a trail of dust, dangerously crossing the floor of the valley under the hot sun and within an arrow's reach. Would courage and valor save the day? Yes, Monument Valley was the biggest stage of them all, and Max Weitzenhoffer has yet to see it—other than in the movies.

But Monument Valley will have to wait because the script has changed, courtesy of the ever-changing face of Broadway and a fountain of curiosity that Max splashes in as if he were still a boy on a summer lark.

The point was driven home recently by a series of events starting with a fundraising trip to New York on behalf of the University of Oklahoma. While he was there, Max dined at Sardi's restaurant for the first time in a long while. It had been his hangout throughout the '70s and '80s, a popular establishment where the theatrical crowd gathered and where he always had the same table. "Sardi's, in the old days, had a system where they put everybody in the theatre business on the left side of the restaurant and the public on the other side," Max said. "They didn't mix the sides up, so it was very communal. You went to dinner there because you knew everybody around you."

His place at the table was cemented in the fact that Max never had to bother ordering a drink because a Martini showed up almost immediately after he sat down. Prime rib was his favorite, with crisped mustard spread over the bones. At one point, Weitzenhoffer and Jim Freydberg considered buying the place before deciding they were not cut out for the rigors of the restaurant business.

After having a surprisingly fine time at Sardi's, Max bit the bullet so to speak and made his way over to Broadway, which he believed no longer held any fascination for him. But there was a musical playing at the Barrymore Theatre that interested him.

The Band's Visit is the story of a group of eight police band Egyptian musicians who wind up by mistake in a remote Israeli town where every day feels the same. They are taken in for the night by Dina, the local café owner who has resigned her desires for romance to daydreaming about exotic films and music from her youth. *The New York Times* called it "one of the most ravishing musicals you will ever be seduced by … and its undeniable allure is not of the hard-charging, brightly blaring sort common to box office extravaganzas.

"Instead, this portrait of a single night in a tiny Israeli desert town confirms a lyric that arrives, like nearly everything in this remarkable show, on a breath of reluctantly romantic hope: 'Nothing is as beautiful as something you don't expect.'"

Weitzenhoffer clearly agreed with those sentiments. He even took it a step further. *The Band's Visit* reminded him of Broadway at its best. "There are no politics in it," he said. "It's about people and relationships; it's about communicating with each other."

The Band's Visit was so moving that it made him second-guess himself as to why he soured on Broadway and New York in the first place. It wasn't really about the colossal expense of doing a show, he decided. It was strictly emotional on his part. "The real reason was Broadway went through this period where all the big shows were about people who were having problems or people discovering they are something they're not," he said. "*The Band's Visit* is simply about love."

If *The Band's Visit* aroused his emotions, what came next was as revealing as a curtain on opening night, except this time the man in the spotlight was not Will Rogers or Dracula or the Phantom. It was Weitzenhoffer himself, the reluctant performer who had to finally admit that after almost six decades on Broadway and the West End deserved a moment in the spotlight. It's a scene from a story that began 30 years ago, not on Broadway but at the Steppenwolf Repertory Company in the windy city of Chicago where playwright Lanford Wilson, who critics credited with being known for his interest in the sound of language rather than in particular themes, and director Marshall Mason had been collaborating off-Broadway for years in what was called *experimental theatre*.

Their latest work was *Burn This* and as Max Weitzenhoffer learned over time, the title would come to hold all sorts of meanings for both the critics and the audience. It was billed as a contemporary comedy that starred Joan Allen as Anna, a dancer and choreographer who falls in love with Pale, a married man with two children (played by John Malkovich). The magazine *Newsweek* called it a play for the tangled '80s where values, energies and desires collide in a hailstorm of ambiguities. That was putting it mildly.

Weitzenhoffer and Freydberg actually got ahold of the production in it what Max described as a moment of pure serendipity. "I was the chairman at Circle Repertory Company and Fred was the playwright at Circle Rep at the time he wrote it so that facilitated things," Max explained. Freydberg and Weitzenhoffer were hooked the moment they saw the play in Chicago and moved it to Broadway almost lock, stock and barrel. "We did make one change because David and I decided it was too long, so we told Mason he had to take 30 minutes out of it somewhere," Max allowed. "Mason and Lanford sat down and cut the play but Malkovich didn't like any of the cuts so he made his own cuts, which neither Mason nor Lanford liked."

Malkovich emphatically broke the stalemate with the same bluntness he often projected on stage. "John said, 'If you don't like the choices I made for the cuts, I'm not doing it.' I don't where the 30 minutes came from but it was Malkovich's decision. But the real moral of the story is that often a really intelligent star like John has a better feeling for the role that he's playing and it's smart for the director to realize it."

Malkovich was clearly born to swagger. When the play hit Broadway, *New York Times* critic Frank Rich called him "a combustive figure on stage, threatening to incinerate everyone and everything around him with his throbbing vocal riffs, bruiser's posture and savage, unfocused eyes." Rich wrote that if "you're going to write a play called *Burn This* as Lanford Wilson now has, Mr. Malkovich is surely the man to fan its flames."

Anna, not Pale, is the central character in the play, but as was the case with Tennessee Williams' Stanley Kowalski, Malkovich takes over the play through the force of his muscular personality. Therefore, it was not accidental that *Newsweek* called Malkovich's entrance onto the stage "probably the most sensational since the young Brando's in *A Streetcar Named Desire.* But Brando's Stanley was decorum itself compared with Pale, the character Malkovich plays. Pale's first speech is the most insanely furious, surrealistically funny riff ever heard on an American stage. Bursting into a New York

City loft shared by Anna (Joan Allen), a modern dancer, and Larry (Lou Liberatore), an advertising art director, the longhaired Pale launches into a supersonic diatribe on his parking problems that leads to … well, that leads to a mainline shot of theatrical adrenaline for an audience that hasn't seen or heard anything to match the sheer theatricality of Wilson's new play in years."

From there the play becomes consumed by the impact Pale and his strongly delivered "F bombs" have on Anna, whose insulated life to that point has focused on two commitments – to her career and to her close friendship with Robby, who was her dancing partner and roommate as well as Pale's youngest brother. As described by *The New York Times*, her career has been unproductive and the extent of her intimacy with Robby has been limited by the fact of his homosexuality. Robby's death forces her to come to terms with the paradoxes of their relationship and once Pale forcibly enters her loft and her life after his brother's death, the stage is set for opposites of the first degree to attract with the intensity of the birth of a planet.

For his part, Lansford called *Burn This* "The best work I've done" even before it arrived on Broadway. "Of course, there are a lot of people who hate it, and that's always good, too. At least I'm not pleasing everyone," he added. There was plenty of evidence to support his conclusion as Pale's opening tirade alone often was enough to drive members of the audience to the exit. "I find people leaving a strain, but that particular one is fun," he said referencing a time at a performance in Los Angeles when a local socialite led her party of four in a determined march out of the theatre. Wilson added that he didn't want to shock people, but at the same time he realized he was writing characters that would not appeal to everyone. "Some people decide whether or not they like a play, or whether or not they are interested in someone's problems based on whether or not they'd want to invite them to dinner," he concluded.

As if to dare the audience to either stand its ground or run in revulsion, Wilson used a line from one his characters as the title: "A writer shouldn't consider he's doing his job unless he writes 'Burn This' at the bottom of every page." Wilson succeeded in getting under the skin and celebrating the free expression of the individual spirit, much to the appreciation of the critics, who said it was mesmerizing, explosive, ferociously funny, powerful, sensational, dazzling and penetrating, among other things. Allen even won a Tony Award for Best Actress in a Play for her performance as Anna. But by the time the fire was out at the Plymouth Theatre on Broadway, *Burn This* failed to deliver at the box office. "We didn't break even." Weitzenhoffer admitted.

He attributed some of the failure to Wilson's raw, over-the-top depiction of the lonely world of displaced persons, using Pale's opening lines as a metaphor for the fine line playwrights and directors walk in order to be true to both themselves and their audiences. "When Pale (Malkovich) first comes on stage, you immediately know that he's an open wound that is unlikely to be cauterized because he's in a rage over the fact that he can't find a parking place in Greenwich Village and every other word is fuck," Max said. "We used to laugh at every show because we'd always have 25 or 30 people immediately get up and leave the theatre because of the 'F' word." Weitzenhoffer eventually realized the play had another problem: In his view, the physical connection between Pale and Anna came off as a bit too chilly for his taste, in contrast to the steamy connection that existed between Malkovich and actress Juliet Stevenson when the play shifted to the Lyric Theatre in London under a different director.

All of that happened a long time ago, not long enough to totally forget, but long enough for him to put the role of a producer into perspective. "I've said this before, but with every production, you as the producer have to face the facts and ask yourself why it didn't work," he said. "Was it because I fucked up or did it not work because the audience didn't see it the way you did? I think when a play goes on stage and it's perfect in your mind and then it doesn't work, well, that's just the way it is."

After *Burn This*, Weitzenhoffer went on to have a lot more success with *The Will Rogers Follies* before eventually turning his sights to London. Lanford Wilson died in 2011 but not before being elected into the Theatre Hall of Fame and the American Academy of Arts and Letters. John Malkovich returned to the States to advance his career as a gifted actor both on the stage and in film. He never returned to London after his role in *Burn This*.

But as is always the case in the theatre, there is always a next act to complete. This time it is one that will bring Weitzenhoffer's five decades-long career on Broadway and in London full circle, much the way he likes to produce plays that take audiences on a satisfying journey. The latest act takes Weitzenhoffer back to London, not as a producer but as co-owner of the theatre that will showcase the work of Malkovich and another famous American playwright who has written something every bit as provocative and topical as *Burn This*. It's hard to ignore the symmetry as the play is slated for the Garrick Theatre in the West End in London, where Weitzenhoffer now owns half a stake. Thirty years ago, Weitzenhoffer took *Burn This* and Malkovich to the Lyric Theatre, in which Max also holds half ownership.

The new play is called *Bitter Wheat* and was written by David Mamet, who like Wilson, won a Pulitzer Prize and honed his craft in Chicago theatrical circles. And like Wilson, he is known for his edgy dialogue, liberal use of profanity and a gift for stretching the boundaries between a man and a woman by strong-arming relationships into the ground. This time Malkovich is returning to London to portray a Harvey Weinstein-type depraved mogul who operates in a hell hole where "bloated monsters devour the young," according to a trailer for the new play.

The Weinstein connection alone will overpower the conversation regarding *Bitter Wheat*, but it is the subplots of a personal nature that fascinate Weitzenhoffer, and rightly so. For example, he relishes the fact that Mamet, a noted American playwright, and Malkovich, a distinguished actor, have chosen to launch the production in London rather than New York. It is a small vindication for Weitzenhoffer, who has challenged the notion that only Broadway could produce thought-provoking theatre.

"I think *Bitter Wheat*, coupled with those who are involved, reflects the history of Broadway and the way the theatre has worked for decades," he said. "When you think things have changed, along comes a play like *Bitter Wheat* which is a step or two ahead of the mainstream and is about something relevant to the times. And I believe it will prove that once again that the theatre is still about the spoken word and exciting actors."

If *The Band's Visit* got his heart beating for Broadway again, *Bitter Wheat* has sent him over the top. "I'm coming back in a different capacity to a time when I had some of my biggest hits and the theme and some of the players are the same," he said. "It's very invigorating." If he is correct, *Bitter Wheat* will also serve as a metaphor for how Weitzenhoffer has patterned his own career – produce a play that is right for the times and pick the best people to perform it, no matter who they are or where they come from, like *The Will Rogers Follies* which came along at a time after the Gulf War I when the audience felt good about America and wrapped itself around the patriotic musical. Or the highly successful musical comedy *The Book of Mormon* which uses contemporary humor to portray organized religion as being out of touch with the times while stressing that religion itself can do enormous good.

"Those shows came at a point in time when the audiences were ready for them," Max stressed. "I'm not sure either would work today. If I would say anything positive about my career it would be that my success has always been about constantly moving with the times and being aware of where we are in the theatre at that moment. I think it's mostly a product of my curiosity, nothing more."

Some say curiosity is what gives the envelope the push it requires to think up a better idea, or a better mousetrap, or whatever is required to test the limits. But curiosity is a hard thing to tap into or predict how far it will extend. Many years ago, back in the Golden Age of Broadway, an award named for legendary 20th Century English musical comedy composer Vivian Ellis was created to recognize and support new musicals. It involved a panel discussion in which pieces of five new musicals were presented and then critiqued by the likes of lyricist Tim Rice, Lloyd Webber and others. At the time, Broadway was riding a streak of mega-musical box office winners —*Evita, Cats, Les Misérables* and *The Phantom of the Opera*—which prompted someone in the audience to raise his hand and ask, "What comes next?"

Rice, who was knighted by Queen Elizabeth II for his services to music in 1994, took on the question. "You know, I don't know what it is coming next, but something's coming," he replied.

Max Weitzenhoffer made his mark in life holding on to that very thought. Long live John Wayne. Long live the theatre.

THE END

The Show goes on

Max's Biography

Aaron Max Weitzenhoffer, Jr.; born October 30, 1939, in Oklahoma City, Oklahoma to Clara Irene (Rosenthal) and Aaron Max Weitzenhoffer.

EDUCATION:

B.A. in Fine Arts from the University of Oklahoma, 1962

Graduate of Cassady Preparatory School, Oklahoma City, 1957

CAREER:

General manager, La Jolla Playhouse, La Jolla, California, 1963–64

Chief of publications, Oklahoma Health Department, 1964–65

Director, David B. Findlay Gallery, New York City, 1965-69

Co-owner, Gimpel & Weitzenhoffer Art Gallery, New York City, 1971-88

President. Weitzenhoffer Productions, Ltd, New York City, 1965-present

President, Seminole Manufacturing Co., Kalamazoo, Michigan, 1989-present

Director of Musical Theatre, University of Oklahoma, 1994–2003

Adjunct professor, University of Oklahoma, 1975–94

Regent, University of Oklahoma Board of Regents, 2003–17 and chairman 2010 and 2017

President, Weitzenhoffer Productions, Ltd., London, England, 1987-present

Chairman, Nimax Theatres, Ltd. London, England, 2005-present

Vice president, New York Dramatists, Theatreworks and Theatre Investment Fund

Board member, Circle Repertory Theatre

Trustee, American Academy of Dramatic Arts

Treasurer, Stage Directors and Choreographers Foundation Inc

Member, League of American Producers and Theatre Owners (member of board of governors), Actors' Equity Association, Players Club, Century Association, Delta Kappa Epsilon, Screen Actors Guild, Friars Club, Society of London Theatres.

AWARDS, HONORS:

Antoinette Perry Award, best revival, 1978, for *Dracula*

Antoinette Perry Award nomination, best musical, 1982, for *PumpBoys and Dinettes*

Antoinette Perry Award nomination, best musical, 1985, *Song and Dance*

Antoinette Perry Award nomination, best play, 1986, for *Blood Knot*

Antoinette Perry Award nomination, best musical revival, 2010,
A Little Night Music

Distinguished Service Citation, University of Oklahoma,1988

Antoinette Perry Award, best play, 1989, *Largely New York*

Antoinette Perry Award, best musical, 1991, for *The Will Rogers Follies*

Inducted into the Oklahoma Hall of Fame, 1994

Laurence Olivier Awards, best entertainment, 2000,
Defending the Cavemen

Laurence Olivier Awards, best revival, 2013,
Long Days Journey into the Night

CREDITS:

PRODUCER WITH OTHERS

Going Up, John Golden Theatre, New York City, 1976

Dracula, Martin Beck Theatre, New York City, 1977

Harold and Maude, Martin Beck Theatre, 1980

Pump Boys and Dinettes, Princess Theatre, New York City, 1982

The Good Parts, Astor Place Theatre, New York City, 1982

Three Guys Naked from the Waist Down, Minetta Lane Theatre,
New York City, 1985

Song and Dance, Royal Theatre, New York City, 1985

Blood Knot, John Golden Theatre, 1985-86

Budgie, Cambridge Theatre, 1988

Largely New York, St. James Theatre, New York City, 1989

Burn This, Lyric Theatre, London, England, 1990

The Will Rogers Follies, Palace Theatre, New York City, 1991–92

Eating Raoul, Union Square Theatre, New York City, 1992

Scissor Happy, Duchess Theatre, London, 1997

JFK: A Musical Drama, Olympia Theatre, Dublin, Ireland, 1997

Also affiliated with the productions of *Bedroom Farce, The Elephant Man,
Equus, Mass Appeal, Passion, Piaf, Rose, Sleuth, Tickles by Tucholsky,* and
Timbuktu!; producer of *Road to Mecca,* Promenade Theatre, *Burn This,*
Plymouth Theatre.

FILM APPEARANCES

Party guest, *Wolf,* Columbia, 1994

Acknowledgments

Sometimes, it is hard to let go, and this manuscript was no exception. Fortunately, my desire to improve it with each passing day was tempered by an unwavering support base. Special thanks go to Max Weitzenhoffer for his cooperative spirit and his engaging mind. Likewise, I am fortunate to have Jim Tolbert for a publisher and Carl Brune as the designer. They are a delight to work with and a pleasure to know.

I also am grateful for the editorial support and encouragement I have received from Mary Heffner, Karen Valentine and Mick Hinton, as well as the insight I gained from Earl Cooper.

As readers will quickly note, *To the Max* has a strong visual element, which relied on the support of a number of people, especially Lynette Lobban of the University of Oklahoma Foundation. In addition, I would like to acknowledge Kaylee Kain, OU Director of Communications; Selena Capraro and Tracy Bidwell, the Fred Jones Jr. Musuem of Art; Sandra Bent and Mary Margaret Holt, Weitzenhoffer Family School of Art; Candace Stimmel, Director, Branding & Licensing The University of Oklahoma; Mike Houch, University of Oklahoma Athletics Department; Kera Newby, the National Cowboy and Heritage Museum; David Leopold, the Hirschfeld Foundation; Mark Swartz, The Schubert Archive; R. Andrew Boose, Trustee, the Edward Gorey Charitable Trust; and Carl Shortt and Todd Stewart, photography.